GRATEFUL FOR THE OPPORTUNITY

A Journey Through Self-Growth

DR. TYLER VAN

ISBN: 979-8-218-21794-5

for those that need a push to keep going

Introduction

The beauty of this text is that it wasn't intended as a means to give advice to others. This writing was initially meant as a way to give advice to myself. This was me speaking to me—day after day. Writing was an escape—a way to feel lighter and de-stress. If it weren't for my cardiac event, I may have never started writing. Real-life scenarios fueled my writing—real emotions were put into every single paragraph. When I felt the universe was testing me, I took that as an opportunity to write—I turned negative into positive. Writing allowed me to keep moving forward. Proofreading was a way to remind myself of what I stood for and the mentality I worked so hard to maintain. Staying positive and motivated requires discipline—it requires effort that should be applied daily. Being able to share my thoughts with others, with the possibility of having a positive impact, is a bonus—a bonus that I will cherish forever.

I made a promise to myself that I would always stay

true to who I am and that I would open up my heart and soul to others. I hope that through this written text I can inspire you to open up and to be your true self daily. I hope I can convince you to not fear what society may or may not think of you. I hope that I can help you realize that it is normal to feel like things aren't going your way—and listen, there might come a time when things truly aren't going your way. What I hope to share is a mindset that will help you evolve—a mindset that will help you feel as though things are always going your way.

I'm not here to shove positivity down your throat—that's not the purpose of this text. While I do hope to inspire you to be more positive, I just hope to inspire you to be real—to be vulnerable and see the beauty in that. I want to help you realize that in the end, it all works out. I want you to understand that you're going to have days that you feel sad—that you feel defeated. I want you to understand that you're going to have days when you are angry at the world and no one can convince you otherwise that it's not the world's fault. You are allowed to have these emotions and these emotions do not mean you are broken. You are not broken and I hope I can convince you of that. I hope I can convince you that being open with yourself and with others will lead to a happier life—a more successful life. Thank you for allowing me to impact your life to some degree.

I am truly grateful for the opportunity.

THE JOURNEY BEGINS

I can't sit here and say I was always this enthusiastic positive person—I'm still trying to be that version of myself. What I can say is that I was always good at being a positive person for others. Whether friends, teammates, loved ones, or patients—I always found myself being positive for them. Why was it so difficult to be positive for me? I still don't know. What I do know is that it's a daily process. Being positive is something that needs to be worked on. To be positive, you need to surround yourself with positive beings. Surround yourself with those that add value to your life—not those that take value away.

Quick story, which I hope can turn into a moment that sparks a change in your mindset—it was the moment that did it for me. I was in graduate school getting my doctorate in physical therapy. I had an exam in two weeks and a huge review the Thursday a week before. On my way to the review, my car stalled on the highway. A 5–6 hour ordeal to get my car towed off the highway and then I had to get another tow to take my car back to New Jersey—this all happened in New York. What a huge inconvenience—I missed the exam review. Fast forward a week to the exam. I am driving to school in New York and my car breaks down again—literally 7 days after getting it fixed. The timing was impeccable. I ended up being close to 2 hours late for the exam after getting a ride to school. Did well, but not great. I was frustrated—I felt unlucky. Just going to stop here quick—the second you start telling yourself you're unlucky, you're trapped. Claiming to be "unlucky" is the biggest trap. Anyway, fast forward to a week after the exam. I had an observation in the neonatal intensive care unit (NICU) and I would later go on to treat in the hospital for one of my clinical rotations. To see family members crying that their child might not make it past 6 months. To see family members struggling to feel hopeful that everything will be okay. That's when my mindset changed. How could I sit there and complain about anything when that was going on in someone's life? My car breaking down, missing a review, and being late for an exam—that was nothing compared to what those families were going through. How could I sit there and call myself unlucky? What I was going through was merely a minuscule obstacle in my life that could be solved. I was lucky for those inconveniences to be the worst of what I had going on. The moral of the story, what may be happening to you is truly nothing compared to what others may be going through. Let me also say that it's okay to feel frustrated, angry, and upset about the inconveniences that happen in your life. It's okay to feel those emotions about things you can't control. But just remember, they are often solvable things—they are often temporary things. More importantly, they are often nothing compared to what could be. Don't dwell—don't sulk. Try to laugh at the inconveniences in life, such as your car breaking down, because at the end of the day, maybe it broke down to prevent you from getting into a major accident later in your drive. You don't know and will never know. That's okay because what you do know is that you are alive, you are reading this, and you are thinking of ways to better yourself.

I truly believe one of the major keys to becoming a positive person and setting yourself up for success is realizing who you are surrounding yourself with. It's also realizing what you expose your mind to on a daily basis. The biggest advice I can give in guiding you in the right direction, and it is something that has helped me tremendously, is to surround yourself with like-minded individuals. Reach out to individuals/brands that you feel have had a positive impact on you/society—ask them questions and look to learn from them. Never be afraid to reach out to someone and ask questions. The worst that can happen is they don't answer—guess what, you'll be in the same position you would have been if you didn't try. So why not try? I've reached out to countless people and brands that never got back to me, but I tried. That's half the battle—trying and giving effort.

You're going to realize that as you grow, your inner circle will get smaller. And you know what? That's okay. There are going to be those that you once held close to you that seem to fade away. People change—change is okay, change is growth. What is important is accepting the fact that those you once held close to you may be holding you back. Those you once held close to you may not be adding value to your life. Remember, surround yourself with those that add value to your life—not those that take value away. Take note of those that only reach out to you when something is needed. If you find yourself constantly reaching out to others to check in, but those don't prioritize checking in on you, it's time to reassess who you invest your energy into. Now I'm not saying to check in on those you love with the intention of receiving—always do anything out of the goodness of your heart. My point is you need to come to terms with your priorities and often those who once were shouldn't be anymore. That seems harsh, but remember people change and change is growth. You're allowed to grow too—

you're allowed to let go. Everyone is going through this thing called life and trying to figure it out. If you spend all your energy trying to help others, but can't help yourself first, what good is that? If you spend all of your energy trying to hold on to relationships that once added value to your life, but no longer do, you'll never grow.

Takeaway points:

1. Surround yourself with like-minded individuals
2. Those that don't add value to your life are taking it away
3. Change is growth
4. It's okay to let go

If there is anything you get out of this, let it be a reminder to just be yourself. Don't live life in the passenger seat—live life the way you want to live it. At the end of the day, you need to be doing what makes you happy. Bet on yourself—go all in. Never stop believing in yourself. Eliminate the "what ifs" and just go for it. Most importantly know your worth—trust me you bring value to this world. Life is too short not to do what you want. If you're unhappy at your job, get a new job. If you're unhappy with where you live, move. Now I get it—it's not always that simple, but if you constantly go through life complacent with where you're at or convincing yourself there is no alternative, you are going to watch life go by. That's not living life, that's observing life. There's always an alternative. The question is, how much effort do you want to put in to obtain that alternative? Take that first step. You'll be a lot happier once you take that first step.

"The worst that can happen is that you fail and end up in the same position as if you did nothing at all."

— Dr. Tyler Van

We live in a society where it is easy to be influenced by others. Now while I think it is beneficial to learn from others and to mold your routine to what other successful individuals do, you can't lose grasp of who you are. Your path will never be the same as the path of someone else. By no means am I trying to convince others to be like me or to follow my exact path, but I hope you can see value in some of the things I've learned from life and am sharing with you now. That's the beauty of life. The ability to take positive aspects or routines that have worked for others and mold them into your own. There's a reason why instruction manuals exist. Those before you have laid the foundation for success, but remember it is just a guideline. Life is always happening and no paths are the same—there's a reason I'm reiterating that. Continue to learn from others, but grow into who you truly want to be—grow into the person you truly are.

Learn to laugh at life. Life isn't all that serious. Aggravations happen—inconveniences happen and, listen, they tend to happen when you least need them to. The second you start focusing on those inconveniences though is when you start heading in the wrong direction. Trust me when I say that if you start focusing on all that is going wrong, all will go wrong. It isn't easy and I've fallen into that trap. I've had moments when I felt I couldn't catch a break—I'm human too. You just need to reassess your mindset and think of all that is good in your life.

Some advice that has helped me get my mindset back on track:

1. Read
2. Write
3. Self-talk

I think the three points above are so beneficial in helping you get out of a funk. I think self-talk is so underrated. Go for a walk and just talk to yourself. Let your thoughts out and see how much lighter you feel. Think about what you're truly worried about and if there is a solution to that worry. I'd say the majority of the time there is a solution to your worry and if there isn't, no sense in worrying because it is what it is.

Someone once told me that life is happening for you, not to you. This stuck with me. It changed the way I approached each day. It prompted me to stop complaining—to truly be grateful for every opportunity that came my way, no matter how big or small. It all starts with your mindset and how you view each aspect of your life. For example, instead of saying "long day, glad it's over" train yourself to say "long day, glad I had the opportunity." You don't have to do anything in this life, but you get to. Do you know how many people would trade their life to be where you are right now? Your job may suck, but you have a job. The traffic to work may suck, but you have a car. Things could always be worse. Learn to maximize your daily potential—to take advantage of each day given to you. There's no reason for any excuses—anyone can accomplish what they want to in this life.

Now, if you're someone who believes that:

1. The odds just aren't in your favor and from the start you were destined to fail
2. You didn't grow up as fortunate as others and didn't have the resources others may have had

then I leave you with this…

"The same boiling water that softens the potato hardens the egg."

I don't know who exactly came up with that quote, but it's an excellent one. Life is what you make of it. Don't be the soft potato—be the hard egg.

Don't be so hard on yourself. You're doing well and you're moving forward. You're growing—mentally, physically, and spiritually. Oftentimes, the biggest critic is the person in the mirror. You can't let that person bring you down. Always talk highly of yourself—always. Too often I see people put themselves down, even as a joke. My advice is just don't do that. You're conditioning your mind in a negative light. There are already too many people that are going to be your critic—you don't need to add yourself to the list. Many are going to talk about you, good and bad. At the end of the day, it doesn't matter. What does matter is that you continue on this journey called life doing whatever it is you want to do for whatever reason you want to do it. If it makes you happy, then do it. You can't let the judgment of others cloud your vision. For me, the lack of motivation from others motivates me more, but I don't want to achieve goals to prove them wrong—I want to achieve goals to prove myself right.

Do it for you.

While I think goals are great, they shouldn't be a reason to get discouraged. I look at goals as more of a road map or guidance, rather than an end point. Even in healthcare, I set goals for my patients, but if the goals are not achieved, progress must continue in a forward direction. Sometimes goals take longer to achieve and you don't get to where you want by when you thought you would. That doesn't mean you just stop and give up—I certainly don't do that with my patients. Of course, I strive to get my patients to hit their goals sooner than later, but life happens and sometimes you need to account for other variables. The same concept should apply to your life and your goals. I think many can attest that life got crazy in 2019 and what you wanted to achieve may have been put on pause. Whether it was getting married, getting that promotion, or traveling the world—you set a timeframe to do so and it didn't happen. That doesn't mean it won't happen and that doesn't mean it's not okay that it didn't happen when you wanted it to. Continue to let goals be your guide. More importantly, when goals are achieved, keep moving forward. Just because you got to where you wanted to, doesn't mean it should be the end.

I'm always looking to do more and achieve more. Your goals are allowed to evolve. Why should goals change and why should you be okay with goals changing? Because life changes and it changes more rapidly than we tend to be aware of. Now, I'm not saying to set goals for yourself and obnoxiously change them frequently—that would be counterproductive. If you set a goal for 6 months from now and when that time comes you're completely in a different place in your life, just know that it's okay for the goal to change. That change should be positive—that change should always propel you forward toward growth. I have set goals for myself and didn't achieve them when I thought I would. That doesn't mean I stopped moving forward—I reassessed, modified, and created a plan to achieve an even better goal.

Goals are more like guidelines than endpoints.

"There's just not enough time in the day"—what a load of nonsense. Another trap we all fall into. I can confidently say I eliminated that phrase from my dialect, but that wasn't always the case. I came to learn that if it's important to you, you'll make time to get it done. Try to replace the phrase "there's not enough time in the day" with "I don't want to prioritize this right now." At least that phrase takes ownership and conveys some sort of structure. To convince yourself that 24 hours is not enough time to get something of importance done is a disservice to yourself—it is a disservice to your work ethic.

If you've taken the time to read this, you're someone who is trying to better themselves. You set aside some time for intellectual growth. It may just be 10 minutes of reading out of your 24-hour day, but you prioritized time to get it done to some degree. This was important to you, therefore you got it done.

Do yourself a favor and list 5 things you want to implement into your daily regimen:

1.
2.
3.
4.
5.

The first step is acknowledging what was important enough to make that list. The next step is organizing your time to get it done—as we discussed, there's more than enough time in a day.

Why is it that we often have no problem investing in companies/individuals, but are so reluctant to invest in ourselves? While there might not be one right answer, fear probably plays a part. I think many people fear investing in themselves won't be worth it—that the time, energy, and even money they put into their dreams will only lead to disappointment. Do you know what's disappointing? Not trying, not betting on yourself, and not believing in yourself to achieve greatness. That's what's disappointing—certainly way more disappointing than someone who bet on themself and didn't achieve their goal. At least that person tried and while they might have not achieved the result, they learned from it. Success doesn't exist without failure. Stop living life complacent and take risks.

One of the best ways to shift your mindset from negative to positive is to get in the habit of starting your day with positive action. Whether that's reading a book, journaling, exercising, meditating, etc.—do something that is going to impact your day positively. What you do first thing upon waking up sets the tone for the remainder of the day.

Here is a glimpse at my morning routine:

1. Wake up at 4:30 AM
2. Gym by 5:00 AM
3. Cold shower
4. 10 minutes of reading/writing

Find your recipe for having no bad days. I found my morning routine to be the recipe that has set me up for no bad days. There's just something about starting your day with positive action that enhances your well-being physically and mentally. I think the earlier you can kick-start your day the better. For me, it's 4:30 in the morning, but for you, that may be different. Once you have a routine that works for you, the next step is staying consistent. Consistency is key—consistency breeds growth. When you accomplish so much early in the morning, you'll start to realize how much time is truly left in the day to get things done. You'll feel this sense of accomplishment and start to see a shift in your mood. You will feel more alert and more in tune with yourself. You will begin to feel less stressed—that your mind is clear and that your thoughts are not as heavy. You will begin to see a positive impact at your job, in your relationship, and most importantly, within yourself.

My challenge to you:

1. Wake up before 6 AM
2. Exercise for 30 minutes
3. Read or write for 10 minutes

Do this daily for 1 week—let me know how you feel.

Negativity is contagious. No one wants to be around someone negative—someone who is constantly complaining about literally every single aspect of their life. Do you know what else is contagious? Positivity. Be positive—people want to be around positive individuals. Don't be the person who no one wants to be around. If you're struggling to feel lucky, to feel like life is happening for you and not to you, pay close attention to the following:

1. Take note of who you are surrounding yourself with
2. Take note of the environment you put yourself in daily
3. Make a list of all the stressors in your life

If you are someone who surrounds yourself with individuals who are not motivated, who don't add value to your life, who complain and just bring the mood down—time to reevaluate who you are hanging out with. If you are someone who works in an environment that is filled with those that show up just to collect a paycheck, gossip, and not truly make a difference—might be time to look for another job. Of course, that isn't always practical, so let me ask you this—do you engage in gossip? Are you there just to collect a paycheck or are you there to truly make a difference and impact your respective field? So, if getting another job is not practical, do yourself a favor by not surrounding yourself with nonsense. Help yourself by not engaging in gossip and by focusing on having a positive impact on others around you. More importantly, don't do it for the money—your misery is not worth the paycheck. Do whatever it is you want to do, but make sure you're happy doing it. Lastly, after you have identified the stressors, come up with a solution to get rid of them—there's always a solution.

I'll never stop stressing the importance of asking questions. You should always strive for answers in life. However, realize that you're never going to have all of the answers and that's okay. Some things happen in life without explanation. The universe just has a way of working sometimes that leaves you befuddled—it sends you down a path looking for an answer that doesn't exist. Those are the instances that you need to let go—those are the instances when you need to accept that you might not get an answer. Allowing your mind to question, dissect, or overanalyze a situation that has no true explanation will just lead you to feel stressed—to be filled with anxiety, sadness, or lack of hope. Sometimes you just need to let life run its course—that maybe, just maybe things truly do happen for a reason. You might not realize the reason at the time, but maybe years from now you will. I think there's beauty in that—I think that's enough to give anyone hope.

Someone once told me, “It’s okay to not have an answer, but it’s not okay to not have an answer to the same question asked twice.” You are never going to know everything, so take my advice and just check your ego at the door. No matter how much reading you do, how much schooling you’ve gone through with whatever level of degree you may hold, you will not know everything. The smartest people in the world do not know everything. There’s a reason why specialties exist—it’s impossible to know everything and if you’ve convinced yourself that you know everything, listen up. Come to terms with the fact that you don’t know everything and it’s not expected of you to know everything. It’s truly okay to not have an answer, but what is important is that you put forth the effort to find an answer. Don’t fake it—be real. It’s okay to say “I don’t know” or “I’m unsure.” I have much more respect for professionals who can admit they do not know and I have even more respect for those that follow it up with “but I will look into that for you.” As you can imagine, there’s no “fake it till you make it" in healthcare so I've learned rather quickly the importance of saying, "I'm unsure about your question, but let me look more into that." Let this concept apply to all aspects of life and all professions in life.

"It's okay to not have an answer, but it's not okay to not have an answer to the same question asked twice." — Unknown

Don't let your ego sway you from learning from others. So many individuals possess a great amount of knowledge and experience that you may benefit from. Don't be embarrassed to ask questions or feel ashamed to do so because you're "expected" to have that knowledge. Do you think just because I possess my doctorate that I don't ask questions? I am constantly seeking to expand my knowledge from all walks of life. I love learning—I ask a ton of questions and look to indulge myself in experiences with others that are going to help me grow. Do you want to know the secret to growing mentally, physically, spiritually, financially, etc.?—help others grow. Your personal growth will skyrocket exponentially the second you start helping others grow. I can almost guarantee you that in the process of helping others, you will learn a great deal and simultaneously help yourself. Give more than you take and watch your life change forever.

Takeaway points:

1. Check your ego at the door
2. Don't be embarrassed to ask questions
3. Help others grow
4. Give more than you take

Learn to enjoy the ups and downs—to laugh when life isn't going your way. You're going to struggle in life to some degree, hate to break it to you. The path to success isn't linear—it rarely ever is, but life is about the journey. Life is about the obstacles you face and the effort it took to overcome them. Who wants an easy path to success? To have to work for it, to grind for it, and to exert every ounce of your being to get to where you want to be—now that's fulfilling. When you get knocked down, get right back up. When you feel the odds are against you, keep moving forward and double down on yourself. When no one else is believing in you, prove them wrong—better yet prove yourself right. Remember, you're doing it for you. When you come out of the struggle, remember why you kept going and how great it felt to get to where you knew you'd be. More importantly, remember how the struggle molded you into the person you are today—that it never defined you, but merely just made you stronger. So, the next time you feel like you're struggling, take a deep breath and remember that the journey is just as good as the destination.

When it comes to struggle, just remember people are fighting battles you may not see—battles that may not be obvious. The person next to you may look happy but might be fighting against a storm internally. You truly never know what someone is going through and the obstacles they face daily. Be kind to others—reach out to those you care about and check in. If you are someone who is struggling, know that it is okay to talk about your struggles.

Know that in doing so you will not only be helping yourself, but you'll be helping someone going through similar struggles too. Take care of yourself because you can't help others unless you help yourself first.

Take a moment and reach out to
someone you care about.

Stop worrying—everything will work out and what was meant to be will be. Let tomorrow's problem be tomorrow's problem. Teach yourself to live in the now. We often focus so deeply on the past or the future. The past has happened, there's no changing it so why dwell on it? Tomorrow isn't promised, so why not enjoy the now instead of worrying about what may or may not happen? Forget the hypotheticals—don't even think about those scenarios. Hypothetical scenarios are a recipe for anxiety and stress. Try to eliminate "what if" from your mind—while you're at it, eliminate "should've," "would've," and "could've" too. Next time you find yourself worrying, set a timer. I'm being serious—sit there and time how many minutes you spend worrying. Take note of the minutes spent aimlessly thinking about stuff that doesn't even matter—stuff that hasn't even happened yet OR may not even happen at all. Take note of the minutes spent aimlessly thinking about what you could have done, should have done, or would have done differently. Guess what—you cannot change what has already happened to you. You've grown since then and what happened molded you into who you are right now. It made you the strong individual you are right now. Just live in the now. There is so much going on in life—don't waste away life worrying. Enjoy all that this world has to offer. Be present—be in the moment. I have spent too much time worrying. I have spent too much time stressing out about things that didn't even matter—scenarios or outcomes that didn't even happen. Better yet, I've spent too much time worrying about situations that ended up working out in my favor. When I realized what was meant to be will be, my life changed. I started to truly live in the now—to focus on what was right in front of me. Do yourself a favor, stop worrying.

"Stop worrying so much about the next part of your life—you're right in the middle of what you used to look forward to." — Unknown

Don't live life with any regrets. Who you were then has shaped you into who you are now. The decisions you made 5–10 years ago meant something at that time. Don't look back and contemplate what you could have done differently. If you would have done it differently you would not be who you are today. You wouldn't have the life you have today—whether you believe it or not, you have a great life. If you're someone who doesn't think so, I hope to convince you otherwise.

For starters, you are alive. You have the opportunity to make the most of this life that you're living. Many don't get the opportunity you do—make the most of today and every day. Be grateful for the opportunity because someone out there would kill to be in your shoes. Someone always has it worse, remember that. There are going to be times when you're going to make bad decisions, you're going to screw up, and you're going to feel like you dropped the ball. Don't let those moments define you. Don't regret those moments, for it's those moments that teach us how to be resilient. Those moments are lessons—lessons that are lifelong and will make you stronger mentally, physically, and spiritually. Don't fold in those moments and don't dwell on them when those moments pass by. Remember, never have any regret—no matter how bad of a decision. Every choice you've made, no matter how good or bad, has brought you to this very point.

Takeaway points:

1. Live with no regrets
2. Be grateful for the opportunity
3. Remember you have a great life—you are alive

If you're someone who constantly puts others before yourself, pay attention. It is important to give more than you take—be generous, kind, and helpful to those around you. I want you to remember though that you can't help others unless you help yourself first. Realize that it's acceptable to make yourself a priority—that it's okay to say no to others. You can't feel guilty about saying no. You're not going to be able to help everyone or fix everyone—it's not realistic.

As a healthcare provider, I found myself always saying yes to others. Patients would come late, show up on days they weren't even scheduled, and ask to come for an appointment during my free time to eat a quick lunch—and I'd say yes, almost always. I wanted to help people—I love helping people. If that meant not eating lunch or staying late to treat a patient, I did it because I constantly put others before myself. I felt as a provider I needed to put myself second, but you can't live like that. Now, I'm not sitting here saying I don't have my patients' best interest in mind—I go above and beyond for my patients and I take pride in that. What I am saying is that there needs to be a fine line between doing what's right for others and doing what's right for you. You can't overwork yourself—even those that care for others need rest. You can't, and you don't need to, carry the weight of the world on your shoulders. You can be generous, kind, and helpful to those around you and still put yourself first. You have to put yourself first—only then will others receive the best version of you.

You can't help others unless you
help yourself first.

As I've mentioned earlier, claiming to be unlucky is the biggest trap—it's a spiral down a hole of frustration, sadness, and stress. Learn to see the lesson in all that does not go your way—to see the good in what you perceive as bad. I want to share some examples of when I felt unlucky, and while I may have felt unlucky at the time, I can see now the value of those occurrences.

I am a former collegiate athlete—I played lacrosse all four years of college. In my junior year, during a walk-through practice the day before a game, I tore my meniscus which required surgery. My season was over—I remember telling myself how unlucky for that to happen during a practice that wasn't even a strenuous one. What an inconvenience to have to travel back home, get surgery, miss class, catch up on all of the classwork I missed, etc. So many thoughts went through my mind. Worrying that I would have to repeat a semester because of missing too many classes. Worrying that the injury would ultimately delay my entry into a graduate program for physical therapy. Worrying that I would never be the same athlete again. At the time I was already painting a picture that was so negative. Long story short, I underwent surgery and everything was fine. Remember how I said to forget the hypotheticals and stop worrying about outcomes that may not even happen?—a perfect example. While at the time I may have felt discouraged, I now can see the value of that injury. Due to that injury, I learned to relate to my patients on a deeper level. I lived it—I went through the rehabilitation process. I now know from both a provider standpoint as well as a patient standpoint. I truly believe that injury helped mold me into the healthcare provider I am today—that's the value.

On October 16, 2022, I experienced a cardiac event. I woke up early that Sunday morning and everything was normal, but by 11:30 AM I felt my heart start to race. I assessed myself and noticed that my pulse was irregular. I proceeded to put a pulse oximeter on my finger and my resting heart rate was fluctuating between 150 to 180 beats per minute (it should be 60 to 100 beats per minute). I called an ambulance as I suspected I was in atrial fibrillation, which was the case. I was given medication in the ambulance to correct my heart rhythm—it didn't work. I was then given medication in the hospital to correct my heart rhythm—it didn't work. I had to be cardioverted, meaning my heart had to be shocked back into rhythm. I'd be lying if I said I wasn't scared. I'd be lying if I said I didn't feel unlucky. I tried so hard to stay positive and to practice what I'm constantly preaching, but at that moment I struggled. I'm here to tell you that you're going to have your moments when you struggle to stay positive—that you feel you're doing everything right and things just aren't working out in your favor. Remember though, you have to take any occurrence and try your hardest to make it a positive. That event happened during a time when I felt like I couldn't catch a break—that event made me feel unlucky. I was going against all that I preach, which led me to write down my thoughts as a way to vent. I can confidently say that the experience I endured led to a positive outcome. Such an event motivated me to be better, not only for myself but for those around me—that's the value.

Learn to see the value in
unfortunate circumstances.

Just a reminder, no one is perfect. You'll have instances when you go against everything you preach to others. What's important is that you remember your core values—you remember what you truly believe in and how hard you've worked to get to where you are mentally, physically, and spiritually. At the end of the day just be real. The moment you do that is the moment you'll start to get back on track—back to who you truly are and all that you stand for.

It's easy to blame others—it's easy to blame external factors when life doesn't go your way. Take ownership and realize that sometimes it's simply your fault. That maybe, just maybe, things didn't go your way due to lack of preparation. That maybe, just maybe, things didn't go your way because you were unmotivated to get them done in the first place. When things don't go your way, you need to ask yourself, "Did I do everything in my power to get the outcome I wanted?" If the answer is no, then go back to the drawing board—take ownership of that. If the answer is yes, well maybe the odds just weren't in your favor this time around, but the beauty in life is that you get to try again—you get to continue to work at whatever it is you want to achieve. As a society, we tend to have such a difficult time accepting failure—we have such a difficult time taking full ownership of being the reason failure happened. You will get nowhere if you consistently blame others, there is simply no growth in that. Use failure as a lesson and move forward.

Now, I can already sense those saying to themselves, "Well what if I am part of a team and my teammates just don't show up? What if they simply don't give it their all and failure ensues?" If you're reading this and an example along those lines crossed your mind, my response to you is this: as a leader, what did you do to help better the situation? Is there anything you could have done to help rectify the situation or increase the chances of receiving a positive outcome? Let's take the workplace for example—I'm sure many of you work in a team setting. Sometimes your coworkers may not give the effort you are putting forth. What's important though is that you step up as a leader to help the situation. If you just sit back and do nothing, you're just as responsible for failing. Even when others aren't doing their part, you can't sit there and blame them. You need to do everything in your power to increase your chances of success. Listen, there are going to be times when you truly do everything you could to get a positive result and it just doesn't happen. What's important is that you tried—at least you can say you tried and gave all of your effort.

Just stop blaming others—start taking responsibility for your actions. Pointing the finger and accusing others is one of the biggest copouts in life. Making excuses is such an easy thing to do—it's such a weak thing to do. Be honest with yourself and recognize when you are at fault. If you become distracted, do you find yourself blaming the one doing the distracting or do you take responsibility for allowing someone to manipulate your focus? Do you see what I'm saying? Start doing some self-reflecting—recognize areas in your life where you find yourself blaming others. There is no way you'll grow in this life if you continue to deflect and avoid taking ownership of your actions. You will never learn unless you can recognize and accept when it is your fault. You cannot run away from your actions—you should not run away from your actions. Mistakes will be made—it is inevitable. You need to own your mistakes—you need to learn from your mistakes. You will become a better individual when you can take ownership of your actions.

Take some ownership—stop blaming others.

There's such a correlation between being an athlete and working for a business. As an athlete, you practice every day to get better, and professionally, the same concept applies. You need to work at it—approach anything in life with the intent of maximizing your potential. How you do one thing is how you do everything, remember that. If you don't give all of your effort when you are practicing, then

I can promise you that come game time it's going to show. If you get in the habit of being lazy outside of work, I promise you that those habits will carry over into the workplace. Practice, practice, practice—whether it's for a competitive game or a work presentation. Try and focus on the small wins as those will get you closer to your vision. Whether you're on the field or in the office, truly give it your all.

I'm someone who is constantly looking to get better—to be a better person, a better clinician, or a better athlete. One of the simplest ways to get better is to seek feedback from others. Be receptive to feedback, embrace it. Often, we get way too defensive when others give us feedback. I love feedback—I want to know what I'm doing wrong or what I'm doing great. How else am I going to grow if I'm not aware of the impact I have on those around me? Be aware of your weakness or areas of struggle so you can improve as a person. Be aware of your strengths so you can amplify them. As important as it is to be receptive to feedback, it's just as important to give feedback. Be constructive when giving feedback—help others around you grow. Help others recognize areas in need of improvement. Help others recognize areas of success—areas in which they are achieving great things. People love hearing that they are doing a great job—people love hearing that they are worthy. Small comments of gratitude and appreciation go a long way—it also helps others become more receptive to feedback in general. Feedback isn't about putting people down—it's about lifting people up. Make an effort to help those around you grow and watch how much you grow yourself. Feedback is such a necessity for growth.

Be receptive to feedback.
Give constructive feedback.
Help those around you grow.

You are going to receive comments from others that are negative. You are going to receive comments from others that weren't meant as feedback, but rather to put you down. You are going to receive comments that were made to see if you were fragile enough to break. Don't break—don't even bend. Recognize that everyone is entitled to their opinion, even if that opinion is about you. Also, recognize that you are entitled to not pay any attention to such an opinion. What others say about you does not define you—you define you. Unfortunately, the more you achieve in this life, the more backlash you'll get. The more you achieve in this life, the more people will have to say about you—good and bad. Do not dwell on the opinions others may have of you. You cannot let the opinions of others make you feel unworthy—you are worthy. You are strong, resilient, and making a difference in this world. You are impacting the lives of those around you and people are taking notice. Let others have their opinions of you, after all, it is their right. What do I do when something negative is said about me? I acknowledge the comment, self-reflect, ask myself if there is any truth to a such comment, and move on. Laugh it off because, at the end of the day, the only opinion of yourself that truly matters is your own. Stop caring so much about what others think of you—about what others have to say about a life they are not living. Be receptive to feedback, but do not let the opinions of others bring you down.

You define you.

It's easy to get discouraged in life when you're not seeing the outcomes you want. When you work so tirelessly to achieve your goals and you feel like you're not making any progress. It can be even more discouraging when someone who puts in minimal effort gets everything they want and achieves everything you've been tirelessly working towards. In those moments, do not get discouraged and continue to focus on you. You can't get caught up in what others are achieving. You can't get caught up in what others are doing or not doing. Worry about yourself and your story. Worry about your efforts and what you are doing to achieve your goals. Is it in our human nature to get jealous? Sure. Will being jealous catapult you down your pathway to success? Obviously, no. Understand that your time will come and it often comes when you least expect it. It will happen when it's supposed to happen—you just need to trust that it will. It will happen if you put forth the effort to make it happen.

Everyone has a story. Be mindful that you do not know everyone's story, at least in its entirety. Be mindful of what others may be going through. Often, we see and judge others by what they put out there—by what is shown on social media. While someone may be portrayed as being happy, they can very well be fighting their hardest battle. When Chadwick Boseman, a legendary actor, was battling cancer, photos were released of him during treatment. No one knew he was battling cancer and when people saw those photos, comments were made about his health—all extremely negative comments. Yet he was fighting his hardest battle and didn't want people to know. He wanted to stay strong for his fans. He wanted that information to remain within his inner circle. The moral of the story is that you should never judge anyone—never assume what they may or may not be going through.

Always look to uplift people—never to bring them down.

There are going to be times when you are judged. There are going to be times when what you are trying to convey is misinterpreted. I'm a loud and passionate person—it's just who I am. I speak loudly—I put my heart and soul into everything I do. Oftentimes, I am judged—my passion is misinterpreted for anger, frustration, or being argumentative. I've been told I come off serious and that I am an intimidating person. Those who know me to my deepest core know that my intentions are always good. Those who know me to my deepest core know that I'm constantly looking to uplift those around me—that I would go to battle for anyone who needed me. Those who know me to my deepest core know that I wear my heart on my sleeve. I've been judged wrongly and I'll continue to be judged by those around me. What's important is that I don't judge—that I continue to focus on myself. What's important is that I continue to live life with the intent of doing good—with the intent of helping those around me. That's how you need to live life—without judgment, with an open mind, and with the intent to do good always.

You're going to go through many ups and downs in life. You are going to have moments you don't even know who you are, but life is about finding who you are. Many set out to be a certain image of themselves or set out to be like someone else, rather than just focusing on being them. Be you—be the best version of yourself and when you think you found yourself, keep going. Continue to evolve—continue to grow. Remember it's okay to change. It's okay to have a different mindset than you did yesterday. It's okay to let go of who you were and mold into who you are becoming. Realize that who you are becoming isn't an endpoint—it's a destination that you'll always be chasing. The chase just needs to move in a positive direction to allow yourself to grow. Right now, in this very moment, you might think you are who you were meant to be, yet 10 years from now you'll be saying the same thing. Trust the journey you are on and continue to grow.

Take a moment to think about all of the times that made you happy. Take a moment to think about all that you are looking forward to. Those moments that have passed and those that have yet to occur give you meaning—they give you purpose. Those moments are molding you into who you are meant to be. Take a moment to think about all that you want to accomplish in this life. You are doing it—you are paving the way. Those moments you look forward to will come, trust that they will come, but for now, live in this moment. Write down all that you want to accomplish in this life and store it away. A year from now, check what you wrote down—you'll be amazed at how much you've accomplished.

The first step in achieving what you want to achieve is believing that you will. You'll never get anywhere in life if you don't believe in yourself. Bet on yourself—take risks and stop playing it safe. Better yet, just show up—half the battle is just showing up. Half the battle is taking initiative and putting forth effort. Don't fear failure—there is no success without failure. Have the confidence to do whatever it is that you want to do. Don't fear the unknown—don't fear judgment. Do what makes you happy and have fun doing it. It is never too late to start your journey—to change direction or go on a different path. You can do and achieve anything in this life. Don't wait for the perfect time—the perfect time is now.

"Whether you think you can or you can't, you're right." — Henry Ford

Not many things are promised in this life—take advantage of every opportunity that comes your way. Be grateful for every opportunity that comes your way. Don't be indecisive—just go for it because time waits for no one. I believe many things keep us from doing what we want—fear, finances, and judgment from others just to name a few. You can't live life with hesitation. You can't live life in a constant state of "what if." Remember how I said to eliminate "what if" from your mind? I meant it.

Money comes back, but time does not. Book the trip—explore what this world has to offer. I can't imagine living a full life and not exploring this world. Network, connect with others, and learn about other cultures—take advantage of the opportunity you get to interact with others. There are so many people in this world full of unique traits and characteristics. There are so many beautiful minds filled with knowledge. Ask questions and learn from others—I try to learn something new every day. I have learned so much from my patients and I'm grateful for the opportunity to come across so many walks of life. I treat every day as a lesson. I don't fear being judged—I don't fear not knowing everything. I take advantage of every opportunity that comes my way, big or small, and I try to maximize that opportunity.

Takeaway points:

1. Take advantage of every opportunity—just go for it
2. If you haven't done so already, eliminate "what if" from your mind
3. Try to treat every day as a lesson

Trust your gut—when all else fails trust your gut. Learn to listen to your instinct. You're going to be put in situations where your mind is telling you one thing and your heart is telling you another, but your gut will be the answer. That feeling you have deep down, that initial feeling you get, that's the answer. Condition yourself to not contemplate or second guess yourself. Do not overthink—do not worry about if you made the right choice. Remember, you are someone who does right by others and is constantly seeking to do good—your gut knows that. Allow yourself to trust that your gut will guide you to do the right thing. There will be a time, probably multiple, when you get backlash for your decision—when others will disagree with the route you decided to take. What is important is that you stay true to yourself. What is important is that you continue to not only do what is best for yourself but for those around you. No decision will ever be the wrong one if you intend to do the right thing. Trust your gut, do what you feel is right, and stop worrying about what others are telling you to do.

When all else fails, trust your gut.

Don’t let your emotions get the best of you. You’re going to have days when you’re experiencing a spectrum of emotions—from anger to happiness. Don’t let your emotions cloud your judgment. Don’t react, rather learn to take a deep breath and process what is happening first.

You're going to have instances when others just really trigger you—that you feel others just can't see or understand your perspective. Now before you react, question if you are seeing THEIR perspective. Question if you are failing to understand what THEIR intentions are. Put yourself in the other party's shoes and try to see the situation from THEIR point of view. A lot of times emotions get the best of us because we feel entitled—that we feel we are deserving of a specific outcome. Often we feel instances have to go our way because that's just how it should be—that there can never be any sort of error made in the process. There's a reason I emphasized "their" previously and it's because we so often fail to view scenarios from the outside in. Handling situations from the viewpoint of others, and not just yourself, becomes extremely beneficial to all parties involved. When you start to accept the fact that mistakes happen and people have bad days is when you'll start to handle situations so much better.

Just as much as you shouldn't react to negative situations, the same can be said about positive situations. We often get so caught up in positive emotions such as happiness, gratitude, and love that we fail to see the reality of the situation. For example, you get a promotion at work and what is the first reaction you have?—wanting to tell others about it immediately. We react, rather than process what is happening. We react and we don't take the moment in for ourselves. Rather than reacting, process what is happening and think about all of the alternatives. What if the promotion gets revoked? Can you imagine bragging to others about your promotion before the contract is even signed? My point is many of us react to the good in our lives before we get to even process what is happening, enjoy it for ourselves, or before it is even a sure thing.

Nothing is a sure thing until it is.

Take 24 hours before answering an email. Take a day to process crucial scenarios. If a response or answer isn't time-sensitive, then take the allotted time. There is no reason to respond to anyone in a state of heightened emotion, whether positive or negative. Ensure that you have mental clarity before any response is given.

Takeaway points:

1. Stop reacting
2. Take a deep breath and process what is happening
3. View scenarios from the outside in
4. Nothing is a sure thing until it is

Stop chasing perfection—it's a never-ending chase. It's a chase that only leads to being over-critical of yourself and others. Too many people are their own worst enemies because of this chase. Many people start to expect way too much out of others because of this chase. I've chased perfection and only found myself miserable. I found myself over-analyzing everything I did. I found myself starting to care about what others may think and that everything I did needed to be perfect because that was the standard I set for myself. You shouldn't care what others think of you. Just be authentic—just be yourself. You can't have this standard of perfection and expect others around you to live up to it. You are going to realize that there will be times when you put your energy into others and it isn't reciprocated. When you start to understand that no one owes you anything is when you start to find true happiness—when disappointment truly starts to fade away. Stop putting so much pressure on yourself to be perfect—whether that's perfect in school, perfect at your job, or perfect in your relationship. What's important is that you constantly put forth your best effort—that you continue to do right by others. Instead of being so hard on yourself and putting yourself down, start to lift yourself up.

Listen to the 5-minute rule, which is: don't stay angry longer than 5 minutes. There is no reason that you should remain angry for longer than 5 minutes. If that's the case, distance yourself from whatever it is that is causing you such anger OR check in with yourself to see if you have a grasp on your own emotions. One way or the other, learn to let go—learn that nothing in this life should have the power to dictate your emotions negatively. It's natural to get angry in the sense that it's normal to be bothered by certain aspects of life, but that doesn't mean those aspects should ruin your day—that shouldn't mean that those aspects get to determine your overall state of being. Have you ever heard a coach say to their players "short-term memory" or "focus on the next play?"—that's how you should approach aspects of life that anger or frustrate you. Athletes that have "short-term memory" or can "focus on the next play" are so successful because they have a grasp on their emotions—they can let go and they do not let external factors bother them. They can focus on the task at hand and perform at their optimal level. Sure, athletes get frustrated and get angry, but the ones that are the most successful let those emotions go very quickly—to the point that nothing negatively phases them. Be like these athletes—move on and do not dwell. Dwelling on whatever angered you does nothing positive for yourself—it's simply wasted energy. Dwelling doesn't do anything for those around you either—it only makes people want to avoid you. The next time something bothers you or gets you angry, take a deep breath and set a timer—don't allow yourself to stay in that state of emotion for longer than 5 minutes. Hopefully, in time, you teach yourself to minimize the amount of time spent feeling this way.

Listen to the 5-minute rule.

You're going to get taken advantage of. You're going to put your trust in people who never deserved it in the first place. You're going to get screwed over. You are going to get frustrated and act out of character because you felt the need to defend yourself. You're going to get angry at the fact that what you would never do to others was done to you. You're allowed to feel hurt, betrayed, and angry, but remind yourself that you can't react. Continue to carry yourself with class. Continue to be the bigger person—you can't stoop down to the level of others. No matter how much you are in the right, you can't get defensive and you can't resort to being argumentative. You are going to find yourself in situations where you get screwed over so badly that you'll sit there asking yourself if it's even real life. It's natural to feel angry and upset in those instances, but you can't let your emotions get the best of you. Accept the fact that sometimes people just suck—that those people are out to benefit themselves with no regard for who they hurt in the process. Accept the fact that maybe they aren't your friend and it was just business all along. You are going to come out on the losing side of things in your life and it won't be because of anything you did wrong. Those times will be the toughest pills to swallow, but use those moments as lessons. Learn what you can from it and move on.

You are going to experience a financial loss. You are going to experience wasted time. Life happens in ways that remain out of your control. It's about how you handle these situations that ultimately determine your happiness, peace, and success. You're going to make bad business decisions. You're going to get screwed out of deals. You're going to get taken advantage of. Your time is going to be wasted and to no fault of your own. These negatives in life are bound to happen, but ultimately what cannot happen is that you let them determine your future. You cannot allow these moments to dictate how the rest of your life will go. These moments cannot, and will not, outweigh all of the moments of financial gain and productive time. Utilize these frustrating moments as lessons. These moments need to be reflected on so that you do not go down that path again. Life is not perfect—it will never be perfect and if you think you're going to make it out of this life without experiencing some sort of negativity like financial loss and wasted time, you're wrong. However, if you treat these moments like lessons, then they will transform into gain. You see, you'll always be winning if you constantly learn. There's no such thing as a bad break if you learn from it. There is no such thing as a loss if you view it as a way to get stronger and smarter—that's how you win the game of life. Do you realize how many successful individuals experienced financial loss, wasted time, and "failure?" Yet, they didn't allow those moments to be categorized as "failure." The ones that went on to create impactful businesses or inspire the lives of many viewed those moments of "failure" or "loss" as gain. The ones that continue to move forward with their life, as happy as can be, don't even give those moments of loss or failure a second thought. They've conditioned their minds to view every negative as a positive, regardless of the severity of the situation. Condition your mind to do the same so that when you experience moments of frustration, loss, or wasted time, you will be unbothered.

You have to want it so badly. You have to relentlessly work at whatever it is you want to achieve. It's funny because as I sit here writing this, in my mind I haven't made it yet—I haven't even scratched the surface of where I want to be in this life. I want more, I want so much more. There's so much that I want to achieve and I know I'm going to do everything in my power to get there—I won't accept anything else. Never get complacent with your life—continue to push boundaries and reach levels you never thought you would ever come close to reaching. When asked what I want to get out of this life, my answer is always to have a positive impact on others—whether personally or professionally. I want to create a community of like-minded individuals who strive every day to be the best version of themselves. I want to create a community of people who wake up every day and tell themselves that they are going to make a difference in this world. I want to create a community of people that are going to impact the lives around them. All I ever wanted was to be surrounded by individuals who make each other better humans daily—that is what I want to get out of this life.

Ask yourself, "What do you want to get out of this life?"

People need to see the value in creating a community. I truly believe that more individual success will come when you start to think more about those around you and how you can improve those lives rather than just your own. Take a moment to think about any sports team. Successful teams are usually comprised of players that do not seek individual accolades, rather they simply want to win. Individual success will occur when you work collectively with those around you—when you put forth an effort to ensure those around you perform better. You will win when you try to help others win. That is the value of creating a community. This concept can be applied to any type of profession. When you start to uplift others and try to propel their success, you will notice a significant increase in your success. I have noticed through working with many individuals, brands, etc. that those that go on to have the greatest impact on others or get the most recognition are the ones who always sought to help others. There is such value in creating a community that no dollar amount can equate.

"You will achieve individual success faster when you strive to support the success of those around you." — Dr. Tyler Van

Life is about connecting and learning from others. Community is everything and you should seek to create your own. You should strive to not only learn from others but to educate those around you. Give back more than what you take from this world. There is something to be said about creating a community of like-minded individuals. It's one thing to be a part of a community, but the fulfillment in creating one is something special. There are so many unique, talented, and knowledgeable individuals in this world. Wouldn't you love to be the one to bring those individuals together? Wouldn't you love to be the reason that these individuals get to enhance their growth? There is beauty behind a group of individuals coming together with a common goal—to learn, to love, to grow, and to help. Someone needs to step up and be the person to create a community, to bring individuals together for a greater purpose, and that someone should be you. Be a leader—be the one that unifies and spreads happiness. Be the one to motivate others to push boundaries—to reach new heights that they never could have imagined reaching. If you ever get so lucky to be a part of a group of individuals that push you, and I mean truly push you, to be the best version of yourself, give back by doing the same for others. Create your community and bring communities together. It becomes one giant network—a giant network of positivity, motivation, happiness, and joy. The best part about creating a community is the process—the process is fun. Meeting new people is fun. Learning is fun. Educating others is fun. The process is fun and will never be stressful if your intentions remain pure. During your process, be grateful for the lives you cross paths with. The privilege to listen to the stories of other human beings, about all they have gone through and the adversity they have conquered, is a blessing. Open up to the world as the world opens up to you. Watch how far you will go in this life when you realize the key to doing so is to just be genuine. If you want people to buy into you, to follow you as you lead, just be genuine. Just be real—it's that simple. Be yourself and practice what you preach. Let your actions, your commitment to excellence, and your aspiration to make a difference in this world be the factors that others buy into. Demonstrate the passion and sincerity that fuels you each day. Let the world see that. Let the world see the lengths you are willing to take to bring happiness to those around you. Watch a community grow because all you did was be real—that all you did was be yourself. Stay true to your ethics and morals—stay true to yourself. There is no way in creating a community if you cannot remain true to yourself. How do you act when no one is watching? How do you act behind closed doors? Who do you become during moments of stress and adversity? That person shouldn't change. If you find that how you act in front of others is drastically different than how you act when you're alone, then you aren't being true to yourself. Remember, there is no way in creating a community, at least successfully, if you cannot remain true to yourself. Put in the work—optimize each day. Do the work not for the recognition, but because you simply crave being better—you simply crave wanting to help others be better. That's the energy that will ultimately lead you to create a community. That's the energy that others want to be around.

I want nothing more than to be the guy that brings people together—that people look to for guidance and help. All I ever wanted in this life was to help people. It's a huge reason why I'm a physical therapist, but I always wanted to help others in ways beyond just physical. I love educating, I love motivating, and I love inspiring. I strive daily to bring people together and I know there will come a day when I have created this huge community of remarkable individuals, all dedicated to being their best versions of themselves—a community filled with human beings looking to enhance each other's well-being. I want to create a community filled with those eager to learn—individuals that crave knowledge. I want to create a community that's filled with those so motivated to help the person standing next to them. I want to create a community filled with happiness and joy. I want to bring people together—it makes me happy.

Community is everything.

What does success mean to you? I think we tend to associate the word success with financial gain and maybe that is what it means to you, but success can only be defined by you yourself. Success is subjective—if you ask 100 people in a room what success means, I promise you that you will not get the same answer 100 times. If you do, please reach out to me because I would love to meet those 100 people. I think many need to sit down and deeply reflect on what success actually means. Think deeply about this so-called favorable outcome you are striving so hard to achieve. Success can be big or success can be small—no metric data can truly define success. Success is determined by you and you only.

Take a moment to write below what your definition of success is:

Motivation needs to come from within. It's great to have external factors that motivate you, but external factors will only get you so far. True motivation lies deep in your soul—it stems from that fire that burns inside of you. You can't rely on others to push you—be the one that pushes yourself to new heights. Believe in yourself—truly believe that you are capable of anything and go for it. The only person that can stop you is yourself. No one is going to get up and get it done for you. No one is going to be able to motivate you better than you can motivate yourself. You're going to have moments you feel weak, you don't feel worthy, or you feel like quitting. You must take your mind to a different place, a place it may have never been before, during those moments. That place is at the core of your being—only you can tap into that place. You must find a way to mentally get there—it's not easy and no one else can take you there but you. You may receive some guidance from others, but ultimately only you have the key to that place. Tapping into that place is imperative—for life and success. If you can't find a way to tap into that place, life will bully you. You will find yourself losing over and over if you cannot find a way to get there, especially during life's toughest moments. Embrace the moments of struggle—embrace those moments and overcome them. You can overcome anything if you can just convince yourself of that. That's all it takes—convincing yourself that you are capable. The mind is strong and the body will follow if you can just convince your body that it can. You can do more than you currently believe that you can. Motivate yourself—dig deep and just get it done. Don't allow quitting to be an option—don't allow yourself to give in to the convenience of copping out. Search for that part of you that is located deep down in your soul—fuel that fire. Push your mind and body to a place you never really knew existed. Allow that motivation to come from within—allow yourself to achieve all that you are capable of achieving.

Whether you want to believe it or not, you yourself are a brand—a personal brand. Your image, your actions, and your beliefs all encompass who you are as a brand. Growing your personal brand, in my opinion, is something that is often neglected and extremely important in achieving success. Your personal brand is your most important asset and it will always be—so why aren't you growing your personal brand? You have all the tools at your disposal to help grow your brand—social media being one of them. It is so easy to network, learn from others, and grow as an individual. Put the time and effort into growing your personal brand.

While I believe social media can be extremely beneficial, it's easy to get lost in it. Don't chase virality—we live in a society where going viral is considered monumental. You can't get caught up in the views, the likes, and the comments—you can't have instant gratification and the attention from others be your driving force to whatever it is that you are doing or want to accomplish. Don't lose grasp of who you are because you are trying to do "what works"—continue to be authentic. There's a fine line between following trends and being yourself. Often, people get so influenced by trends and what is working for others that they completely lose originality. Remember, you are allowed to see the value in what others are doing and take what you need, but let that be a guideline. You are allowed to go with the trends to help propel your personal brand forward but don't lose sight of who you truly are. Do you see what I'm saying?

Building a personal brand takes a lot of work—more than people tend to realize. It can be stressful and frustrating at times. You can't let "algorithms" dictate your mood—trust me I've been there. There have been times that I put money, time, and effort into content only for it to not even get recognized. Building a personal brand is a business and it can be stressful trying to maximize your return on the time and effort put into each piece of content. Although building a personal brand is a business, I saw the most success when I stopped viewing it so much as one. The second I started to just have fun with it is the second I started to see more success. When I started to just be myself and not treat it as "work" is when I gained more exposure. That is when I started to truly network and get in contact with not only some amazing individuals, but amazing brands.

I'm telling you right now if you're solely in it for the money you'll never make it. If your sole purpose in networking with individuals or brands is to receive free products, then you need to completely change your mindset. You should want to work with a brand because you believe in the people that have created the brand, you believe in the product, and you believe in the community that the brand has created. Remain genuine—you will see a lot more opportunities arise if you remain genuine. Building a personal brand shouldn't be about monetization—it's about having a positive impact on others. If you focus more of your time and energy on having a positive impact on those around you, I promise then that the money will come. I was never in it for the money. I wanted to grow my personal brand because I truly enjoyed networking and learning from others. I wanted to be around like-minded individuals. Anytime I began to feel discouraged or stressed about building my personal brand, I reminded myself not to treat it as work and to remember the reason I got into creating my personal brand in the first place. Building a personal brand was a way to escape from the stressors in my life. You can't allow building a personal brand to be a stressor—it's supposed to be fun and a way to escape from stress.

Don't stress—just have fun with it.

I'm going to share with you one of the easiest ways I grew my personal brand. Like I've said before, it was never about the money to me. I simply wanted to connect with other amazing individuals and brands. I came across a brand that was liking a lot of my content on Instagram, so I messaged them. I simply said that I was interested in collaborating and showcasing one of their products. They agreed and sent me a contract—it was my first ever contract through social media. I wanted to impress this brand, so what I did was I hired a professional videographer to film what was asked of me—who by the way I randomly messaged on Instagram. Not only did I do this, but I over delivered and didn't ask for any compensation from the brand. Furthermore, I knew that if my videographer crushed the content it could lead to future business, not only between him and myself but between him and the brand we were filming for. Don't you just love when everybody wins? They were beyond impressed and this led to future contracts between myself and the brand. I did this with a ton of brands and did so much work with my videographer, who I now consider a close friend. I continued to give exponentially more than what was asked of me and never asked for a dollar amount. It was a win-win in my mind—these brands got free advertisement, I got exposure which led to growing my personal brand, and most importantly I was able to connect with awesome people. If I wanted to potentially work with a brand, I would have videos professionally filmed showcasing that brand—I would film, tag them, message them, etc. with the hopes of potentially getting a response and I'll be honest with you, I got a ton of responses. Want to know why? Because people want what benefits them. What brand is going to turn down free advertisement? Not only that, but you are literally telling the brand you are invested in them without asking for anything in return. In the process of doing this, you are demonstrating commitment, passion, drive, and creativity—all aspects brands look for in a partner. I truly believe I gained so much success and traction in connecting with other brands because I stayed genuine—I didn't chase the money or the free merchandise. I did it for all the right reasons—the benefits, like getting paid, came later. If you learn anything from what I just described above, it should be that being genuine goes a long way.

If you're interested in working with other brands, my biggest advice is don't just seek the product—look closely at those who stand behind the product. The network of individuals working with the brand you are interested in means way more than the product that such a brand provides. I work with the brands that I do because I not only believe in the products and utilize the products daily, but I believe in those who endorse the products. I believe in the network of individuals who are a part of that brand. All I ever wanted when choosing brands to work with was to be part of their network of individuals. I wanted to learn, grow, and have a positive impact—I wanted to be a part of a movement and their community. I wanted to get in contact with some of the best in the business—to not only learn from them but to show them that I could be a positive asset to their brand and community. So, while believing in the product and knowing that you will utilize it daily is important when choosing to work with a brand, remember to take a look at the network of individuals working with the brand. It's the network of individuals that means the most.

Network. Network. Network.
Learn. Learn. Learn.
Grow. Grow. Grow.

One of the easiest ways to create content to help grow your personal brand is to simply film what you do daily—there's no need to complicate things. If you're someone who wants to grow your personal brand by filming content, but don't feel like you have enough time to do so, then simply filming what you do daily is a great start. By doing this, you're not going out of your way to devote time, and even effort, to creating content—you're just living your life and documenting it. People want to believe in the product before buying it and in this case, YOU are the product. Convince others that who you are, what you stand for, and your message is going to positively benefit their life. That's why I believe if you live out a positive lifestyle and your focus is on having a positive impact on others, then building a personal brand will be that much easier. If you stay true to yourself and just continue to be you, your personal brand will grow.

I want others to buy into me as an individual first before buying into me as a healthcare professional—that's why the majority of the material I put out on social media is about my life and who I am as a person. I don't want to be defined by my profession exclusively—I want to be defined by everything that makes me who I am as an individual. I want others to know that I have a good heart, a good soul, and that I put maximum effort into everything I do—that as a human being, I am genuine and kind. If others will trust me as a person, then I know they'll be more likely to trust me as a doctor of physical therapy. Yes, I am Dr. Tyler Van, but I am Tyler Van Benschoten first. I want the world to see all that makes me who I am.

You're going to have people that question what you are doing—people that are going to tell you to go a different route or completely change up what you are doing. It is in those moments you need to listen to your heart and believe in yourself. Trust your plan and your vision because quite frankly, no one is going to understand your vision like you do. I've had so many people question why I don't put out more educational videos for physical therapy and why I spend my time filming lifestyle content. As explained above, I want others to buy into me as a person first before buying into me as a professional. I want to appeal to a larger demographic and not just narrow my audience to those seeking rehabilitation advice. I felt my course of action was the best way to connect to a larger audience and to the multiple brands I was eager to work with. And honestly, I just enjoy filming lifestyle content—it makes me happy and it's fun. You don't need to waste your energy explaining to others why you do the things you do. There could be this complex rationale and an entire strategic gameplan behind your actions or it could be that you just enjoy doing those things. Regardless, you don't need to explain yourself to others—remember that.

While you don't need to explain yourself to others, don't be close-minded and shut people out—listen to the opinion of others. What people have to say can be beneficial to you and eye-opening to you as well. Continue to be receptive to feedback and use it to grow as an individual. You don't need to agree with others, and certainly should not change who you are for others either, but you need to continue to have an open mind.

"One of the major keys to success is maintaining an open mind." — Dr. Tyler Van

Nobody cares, work harder. You could have done this, you should have done that, or you would have done this differently—nobody cares. You cannot change what you cannot change. There is no sense in whining, complaining, or blaming—it's all just wasted energy. You can do everything right with maximum effort and things can still not go your way—nobody cares, work harder. You can't sit there and beat yourself up. Go back to the drawing board, find a better solution to the problem, and go for it. The number of times I have said to myself, "Ahh if I just would have done that differently it would have worked out," but guess what? I didn't do it differently, so why even bother talking about it? I realized it was just wasted time and energy to even think about what could have been. And to be honest, no one wants to hear it—truly no one cares I hate to break it to you. People care about results—businesses care about results. No one cares about the hypotheticals. Don't you find it exhausting to talk about what could have been? I can tell you right now it certainly is exhausting to hear about. Discussing, dwelling, and reiterating what could, should, or would have been is just draining energy from yourself and those around you. Have that mentality that nobody cares and all that's left for you to do is work harder.

Nobody cares. Work harder.

I don't even bother discussing with others anymore how close I got to the result I wanted because, at the end of the day, it didn't happen. In my mind, anything short of the desired result is a failure. Who wants to brag about failure? Not me. Sure, I'll open up about my failures with the intent of teaching others what not to do or to motivate others to keep going, but I don't go out of my way to embrace how close to the desired result I got. When you start consistently talking about how close to the desired result you got is when you start to accept failure. That is when you start to accept mediocrity. That is when you begin to get complacent with where you are in your life. Never get complacent—continue to have that fire burn deep within you to want more in this life. You should want to do everything in your power to get the most out of this life you are given.

"Anything short of the desired result is a failure. Don't accept failure." — Dr. Tyler Van

I graduated with my doctorate in physical therapy in 2019—6 months later the pandemic happened. I had so many plans for myself, whether personally or for my career. I had spent the last 7 years in school and many things I didn't get to do while in school I planned on doing in 2019 once my career started. It was completely disheartening that everything I had planned to do I wasn't able to do, but instead of feeling bad for myself, I thought about what others were going through and how much worse others had it. The world was completely upside down. People lost loved ones, people lost their jobs, people struggled financially, and people struggled to provide for their families. I kept saying to myself, how could I complain about the path I was now on with my life and my career when so much worse was happening to others? I reminded myself to stay grateful for the life I was given.

I had all these plans of traveling the world, networking with others, and growing my social media presence, but there we were living in isolation. Like I've said previously, sometimes you just need to go back to the drawing board and find a better solution to the problem. I used that crazy time in our lives to focus on myself—I mean, not for anything, at that time I wasn't even around anyone else other than my family. I began to find a new love for running. As a collegiate athlete, I hated running—I always viewed running as a punishment. Gyms were closed, so I used that time to fall in love with a different style of working out, which consisted of a lot of bodyweight movements and long-distance running. I began to share my workouts on social media, which led to others reaching out regarding them. Slowly, but surely, I was networking with others. Sure, that kind of networking was not what I envisioned, but I was networking and that's what mattered.

My point is there is going to come a time in your life when you feel all of your plans are put to a stop and it won't be to any fault of your own. Your plans and all that you have worked hard for will be halted due to external factors you cannot control. Rather than dwelling on what you cannot control, come up with a way to yield a positive result. I learned a lot about myself during 2019. I learned that I needed to shift my mindset and having a positive outlook on life was a daily process. I learned that having a positive attitude is not something that is achieved overnight and when you think you've achieved it, there is still more work to do. I learned that anything worthwhile in this life takes time and effort—nothing worthwhile comes easy. Learning all of this about myself was a positive result. If I can help others in any way by sharing and talking about my experience, well then that's a positive result too.

Takeaway points:

1. Don't dwell on what you cannot control
2. Having a positive outlook is a daily process
3. Nothing worthwhile comes easy

There are going to be days that you don't want to get out of bed—that you feel completely unmotivated to do anything. Remind yourself that life is happening for you, not to you. Remind yourself that it's not "I have to get up," but rather "I get to get up." This simple change in your mindset will make a huge difference. Wake up and be productive. You don't need to go all out every single day, but you can't allow time to pass by while you sit there doing absolutely nothing. Put forth some effort into bettering yourself and those around you.

I want you to realize that rest and doing nothing are completely different things in my mind. Rest is recognizing that your mind and body need time to recover to perform at an optimal level. Rest is a process with the intent of wanting to be better and do better in the future—for yourself and those around you. Doing nothing is being lazy and having no intention of maximizing your potential to any capacity. Now if you're going to rest, then truly rest. Rest while overthinking and stressing about things you could be doing isn't rest—that is what we call sitting there doing nothing. Rest is taking a day off from exercise with the intent of trying to recover for tomorrow's strenuous workout. Rest is giving yourself enough hours of sleep to be able to perform to the best of your ability at your job the next day. Rest is sitting down, reading a book, and allowing your mind and body to unwind. Doing nothing, on the other hand, is sitting down and contemplating what you could be doing to get better.

Rest vs. Doing Nothing

1. Rest is a process with the intent of wanting to be better and do better
2. Doing nothing is being lazy and having no intention of maximizing your potential

Don't just exercise your body—exercise your mind. You cannot neglect your mental well-being. Read, write, meditate, listen to podcasts, or perform puzzles—keep your mind sharp. Prevent your mind from focusing on the stressors in your life. Pick up an old skill and see how good you still are. Pick up a new skill—work at it and try to master it. Exercise your mind daily.

When I began to read and write daily, I noticed my anxiety decrease significantly. I began to notice that my sense of worry wasn't heightened. My whole mood and outlook on life began to shift when I started to read and write daily. Think of your mind as a processing unit—what goes in gets processed, downloaded, and then you as the individual portray whatever was processed. So, if you read and listen to garbage daily, garbage being material that has no value to your life, then you are going to portray just that. You are going to wear down your mind—your processing unit. It's imperative to consume such material that is going to be beneficial to your life. Now, just as much as your mind can consume material, it can get rid of material as well. Write down your thoughts—write down all of your worries. Think of this as your mind, your processing unit, deleting all unwanted material—you are freeing up storage for material that is going to benefit you. You want to keep your mind, your processing unit, as fresh as possible for as long as possible. Read material that is going to motivate you. Read material that is going to teach you how to grow mentally, physically, and spiritually. Write down all of your worries daily and see how much lighter you feel. Write down tasks that need to get done, rather than consistently thinking about them on a second-by-second basis. Write it all down, free your mind, and stop worrying.

Just please stop worrying. You're going to look back on all of those times you worried and realize it was all a waste—a waste of time and energy. There is no sense in worrying. A lot of the time you spend worrying is about an outcome that won't or didn't even happen. Get out of the habit of fixating on hypotheticals. Get out of the habit of getting lost in your thoughts. Get out of the habit of being worried about what others think because let me tell you, what others think of you does not matter. Think about your health—both your physical and mental well-being. Worrying only affects both negatively. Not worrying can be difficult, but you need to start trying to stop. You cannot allow your mind to fold to negative thoughts. There is so much to be grateful for and so much to be proud of. There is so much to look forward to and so much to experience in this life right now. Do not worry—you are right where you are supposed to be. All that is meant to happen will happen. You are only capable of controlling your actions, so stop worrying about the actions of others. Stop worrying about the inevitable—if it is going to happen, it is going to happen.

Overthinking can be a blessing or a curse—it is up to you to determine which one you make it. I for one am an overthinker. I've turned it into a blessing by using my tendency to dissect situations and overanalyze to help my career. I am extremely analytical regarding my choices in my field and have used what I thought was a curse to maximize patient outcomes. Overthinking has led me to keep busy—to indulge in many different things because it helps keep my mind at peace. It has led me to try new things and focus my mind on aspects that create positivity. Overthinking has led me to write. Overthinking doesn't need to cripple you. You can turn what you thought was a curse into a blessing. You can use overthinking to create opportunities for you. Once you start realizing how overthinking can be used for good, you'll start to sense yourself overthinking less in scenarios that do not add value to your life. Your mind will become more at peace. You will begin to feel less anxious about the world around you. You will begin to feel less upset about situations that do not matter. You will begin to stop second-guessing yourself and the choices you have made. You will begin to stop hyper-fixating on words others share with you—you won't waste time pondering about what was meant by what was said. You will begin to just live your life the way it should be lived. Become at peace with your mind. Overthinking doesn't need to be a bad thing and just because you are an overthinker doesn't make you less.

Overthinking can be a blessing or a curse.
What are you going to make of it?

Invest in your health. Take care of your mind and body. Go to physical therapy, hire a health coach, speak to a therapist, or see your primary care physician. It is way too often that people address issues after the fact—take care of yourself now before issues occur. Take care of yourself and maximize your potential. You should never neglect your health, physically or mentally.

Preventative care is so pivotal to living a healthy life. People always ask me why I see so many specialists if I'm healthy and the answer is that I want to stay that way. I want to ensure that year after year I am as healthy as I can be. I go for yearly screenings, I consult with other practitioners, and I read up on the latest research to implement into my training regimen. I am constantly seeking ways to improve my health and maintain a healthy lifestyle. More importantly, as a healthcare practitioner, I feel it is my duty to practice what I preach. Go for yearly screenings, get bloodwork done, look at your family history, and take note of what you may or may not be at risk for—do your part. Take care of yourself now and do not wait for issues to start occurring.

Movement is medicine—it's free and the best addiction there is. It's crazy to me that there are people out there that aren't addicted to movement—that aren't addicted to exercise. I can't fathom how people are not addicted to longevity—that they're not addicted to maximizing their time spent on this planet. I truly have a hard time grasping this. Implement some form of exercise into your daily routine, preferably in the morning. The feeling you get when you start your day with positive action is like no other. Not only will you reap the benefits of exercise, but you are setting yourself and your day up for success. Exercise with a purpose—exercise with intention and a goal in mind. Often, people exercise with no intention and no plan whatsoever, which ultimately leads to not maximizing their full potential. While some form of exercise is better than no exercise, doing so with a purpose will lead to significantly better outcomes.

Learn to listen to your body. You don't need to go crazy every day—you don't need to push your mind and body to its absolute limit daily. You are allowed to rest. Remember there's a difference between rest and doing nothing. Start to implement active recovery into your regimen. Something as simple as going for a walk can be beneficial. Walks are so underrated—there are plenty of physical and mental benefits from going on a walk. Walks are great for cardiovascular fitness, weight control, enhancing energy levels, and allowing yourself to clear your mind. No one knows your body like you do, so listen to it. When you are in pain, sick, or simply just exhausted, give yourself a break. You don't need to be so hard on yourself. Your body needs rest for recovery and growth. You work hard and you know you do. Stick to your plan, but learn to listen to your body.

Health is wealth.
Movement is medicine.

You cannot live your life in fear. I know it is easier said than done, especially for those who have experienced a traumatic event, but you cannot live your life in fear. Life is too precious and too beautiful to not live your life to the fullest. You can't live your life with hesitation or with the mindset that something is bound to go wrong—that something bad is bound to happen. You must live every day like it is truly your last.

After I experienced my cardiac event, I was scared. I feared that I would start to live life in this constant state of worry—worried that it would happen again or something more extreme would happen. I found myself constantly assessing my pulse—fearing that at any moment it was going to happen again. I'll admit, at first, I was really worried, but as time went on I got better. I was able to overcome that state of worry and remind myself that I cannot live life in fear. I reminded myself that I would not allow anxiety or fear of it happening again to cripple me. I reminded myself that by assessing my pulse second after second, I was only conditioning my mind to stay worried. You cannot do that to yourself. Find ways to stay strong and move on. Overcome any hurdle or obstacle in your life. Have I had days when I've worried about my heart? Sure I have, I'm only human, but I won't allow what happened to not let me live my life to the fullest.

You can't let worry hang over your head. You can't let this sense of worry prevent you from doing everything and anything you want to do. Just because something traumatic happened to you does not mean you cannot overcome it—it does not mean you can't live the life you always dreamed of living. Whatever it is that you are worried about or that you fear, just know it does not define you. You are strong physically, mentally, and spiritually. You are going to be put in situations that make you feel scared, worried, or fearful, but you must remind yourself that you are strong. You can overcome anything if you thoroughly convince yourself that you can.

More people need to get comfortable with being uncomfortable. Why? Because life can get extremely uncomfortable sometimes and the more comfortable you are in those scenarios, the more success you will have with such scenarios. One of the reasons I engage in some form of cold therapy daily is to train myself to get comfortable with being uncomfortable. When you first start to take cold showers or take ice baths, your mind and body want to freak out. Over time, you train yourself to stay calm. This translates to everyday life and how you respond to stress. Whether that stress is from work, your relationship, or if you're battling anxiety or depression, you are training your mind and body to respond more optimally. I believe that cold therapy has helped my mental state tremendously—I believe my anxiety has decreased since engaging in cold therapy daily. I believe cold therapy gives me a sense of feeling more alert and a sense of mental clarity. It has trained me to respond to stressors more optimally. Cold therapy has helped me get comfortable with being uncomfortable.

Cold therapy doesn't need to be your way of getting comfortable with being uncomfortable, but I think many people need to throw themselves into scenarios they normally would not. Do you hate public speaking? Go out and give a lecture to a small group of individuals. Do you hate heights? Go take a rock-climbing class. Do you hate distance running? Start training daily to build up on how long and far you can run. Life is truly about throwing yourself into scenarios that you are not comfortable being in. Doing so is one of the best ways to grow as an individual. You will start to feel more confident, not only in uncomfortable scenarios but in yourself as a human being. You will begin to feel a sense of happiness and fortitude because you were able to overcome uncomfortable situations. Put yourself out there and see the benefit of being put into uncomfortable situations. When you train yourself to deal with those situations to the best of your ability, you truly become unstoppable and set yourself up for the most success.

Get comfortable
with
being uncomfortable.

Do hard things—push yourself to your limit and when you think you've found it, think again because you have no limit. You won't know what you are capable of unless you continue to push boundaries. Do hard things, especially in the morning. Doing hard things in the morning makes the rest of your day feel easier—it makes anything else in life feel easier. Once you accomplish a hard task, especially to start your day, you will feel unstoppable moving forward. You will begin to notice a change in your mood, a change in your work ethic, and a change in how you approach life. You will begin to notice how unbothered you become by the little things in life. You will begin to notice that any obstacle thrown your way will no longer be an inconvenience or a difficult feat, but rather a simple task that needs to be navigated. Your whole mindset will shift. What you once considered difficult or a nuisance will become such an easy part of your day. Nothing can stop you once you prove to yourself what you are truly capable of. No one can affect your mood once you have that sense of accomplishment—that sense of pride. You should want to challenge yourself—you should be eager to see how far you can push your mind and body. Don't be complacent with easy—easy won't facilitate growth. Do hard things and do them often.

"If you climb mountains in the morning, how easy walking through the valley will feel in the afternoon." — Dr. Tyler Van

Be consistent—you will notice a massive change in your life when you start becoming consistent. Whether it's going to the gym, reading, or waking up early—whatever it is you decide to do, do it greatly and consistently. I'm a firm believer that if you stay consistent, you will get better each day—even if it's just 1% better. Remember, consistency is key and consistency breeds growth. Just imagine how much growth can occur if you do things consistently every single day—your actions will compound over time. Understand that it's not just about physical growth either—find ways to grow mentally and spiritually as well. I consistently perform a 2-minute plank every single day. I consistently take cold showers or get into an ice bath every single day. I make it a point to conduct both activities daily for reasons that are far beyond physical benefits. It's about being disciplined mentally. It's about doing something that makes me uncomfortable and learning how to mentally cope with that stressor. I take my mind to a different place when I am performing the 2-minute plank or when I'm engaging in cold therapy. It's like an out-of-body experience or a form of meditation (at least for me) if you will. Both actions have allowed me to grow mentally and both take less than 10 minutes to perform each day. I pray daily and I write down what I am grateful for daily. This has allowed me to grow spiritually and to shift my mood into a positive light. Again, such actions take less than 10 minutes to perform each day. You will become such a better individual, especially for yourself, if you make it a point to stay consistent. Staying consistent can be a challenge in itself, but being consistent is what transforms what once felt like a chore into a habit. Whatever you choose to do consistently will become second nature—then you will find yourself thinking of other ways to get 1% better each day. Next thing you know, all of these consistent actions have compounded exponentially over time. There's something fulfilling about performing an action consistently and being able to prove to yourself that you were able to do it daily. Being consistent requires discipline and it requires effort. Being consistent builds character—being consistent facilitates growth.

"It's no longer a chore when it becomes habitual."
— Dr. Tyler Van

Make an effort to acknowledge those around you. When you walk by people say hello and ask how they are. We live in a world where people struggle to walk by each other without taking out their phones. Have you ever noticed that? When walking by someone in public they immediately resort to reaching into their pocket to check their phone. As a society, we have developed this sense of awkwardness being around other human beings—we struggle to even make eye contact with those around us. I try to make an effort to say hello to those I walk by in public. Not only do I do it because I believe it's the right thing to do, but I know the importance of feeling seen and feeling acknowledged. Many people struggle to feel that they possess any amount of importance or worth. I think many people don't realize the power of smiling at someone and saying hello. I think many people don't realize how asking a stranger how they are doing can go such a long way. Imagine how you have felt when those around you didn't check in on you to see how you were doing—when those you consider loved ones didn't take the time to ask how you have been. So now realize that you, a stranger, showing a sense of concern or acknowledgment to another human being can change that person's day. That you, a stranger, putting forth an effort to ask someone how they are can make them feel important or worthy. It's sad to see that those around you act surprised when you say hello to them. The world doesn't need to be this way and it all starts with you making an effort to acknowledge those around you.

It's as easy as saying, "Hello, how are you?"

Surround yourself with people who truly understand you—people who accept you for who you are and all that you are worth. Surround yourself with people that constantly look to lift you up because they know how much you try to do the same. Surround yourself with people that encourage you and motivate you to be a better person. Surround yourself with people that accept you for you and see the goodness in your soul. There is going to come a time in your life when you realize you need to separate yourself from certain people. There are going to be people you once considered close friends that no longer add value to your life and as harsh as that sounds, it's the truth. Those people are the lives you simply outgrew. Just because you outgrew those people doesn't make them bad people and it doesn't make you better than them either—it just means that you are now on a different path in life. Continue to surround yourself with people who are going to make you better, even if it means going on a different path.

I hope you get lucky enough to find that special someone that believes in you to their deepest core. I hope that you find that certain someone who during your darkest of times looks at you and sees the light. I hope you find someone who no matter what will always motivate you to be a better person—that will stick by your side through the toughest of times. I hope you find that special someone you can say you love with all of your being. It's tough not feeling understood—no one should feel that way. When you find that someone, this feeling will disappear because, for the first time in your life, you will feel understood in your entirety. For the first time in your life, your mind will be at ease because nothing else will matter knowing you have that someone by your side. We cross so many paths in this life—so many that have an impact on us and so many that we have the opportunity to impact as well, but nothing will compare to the impact you and your special someone have on each other. I hope this person teaches you to be vulnerable—that this person teaches you it's okay to be sensitive, to express emotion, and to not have to be so tough for the world all the time. I hope this person teaches you that it's okay to lift the weight that you feel so obligated to carry all of the time off of your shoulders. I hope this person shows you that you don't need to do it alone—that it's okay to ask for help. I hope you find this someone who brings the best out of you—someone who reminds you daily about how great you are. Nothing in the world will compare to this person—crossing paths with this person will be a once-in-a-lifetime opportunity and you'll know when it arises. You will have this feeling you never experienced before—a feeling you will struggle to even put into words. When you meet this someone, you will feel as if they've known you for your entire life. You will feel as if they know more about you than you even know about yourself. It's a crazy feeling that I hope everyone gets to experience. You deserve to experience it and when you do, be grateful for the opportunity you had to meet your someone.

Smile. Be happy. You deserve to be happy. You deserve to go through life enjoying every day. Smile not only because you deserve to, but because smiling is contagious and with that positivity spreads. A smile is inviting. A smile lets others know that you are open—open to thoughts, feelings, opinions, and wisdom. A smile lets those around you know that you are winning at life. Your entire demeanor can be portrayed through your smile—you can't fake a genuine smile because that's exactly what it is not; genuine. Your smile is powerful and it's unique. Your smile is more than just a physical attribute. Your whole mood can be shifted through smiling. Why? Because smiling is contagious. By smiling you lead others around you to smile—to be happy. When you surround yourself with happy individuals, you tend to be happier—it's a beautiful cycle. There is no reason that people should go through their days not smiling. Everyone deserves to smile and be happy.

Smile at the non-believers. People are going to doubt you and you just need to keep believing in yourself. When people doubt you, it should fire you up—not because you want to prove them wrong, but because you want to prove yourself right. Do not let the non-believers have the ability to get you to feel discouraged. The doubters cannot, and will not, have the power to dictate your happiness. They cannot, and will not, have the ability to take away your smile. Everyone is a critic—everyone is going to have something to say about your actions, your mentality, and even your goals. When negativity is thrown your way, when the critics start chirping, just smile and keep moving forward. You are going to go through this life experiencing a lot of doubt from others—you cannot let that turn into self-doubt. You are going to go through this life encountering those that do not want you to succeed, but remember there are plenty of those that do—so smile. Life is too short not to smile—to spend your days sulking, frustrated, or upset. There is too much in this life to be grateful for. There is too much in this life to enjoy. Life is pure. Your smile is pure—so smile.

You do not owe anyone anything. Let me repeat that: you do not owe anyone anything. The only person you owe it to is yourself. Realize that you cannot sacrifice your time and your happiness for others. It's that simple. You cannot go through life feeling guilty because you put yourself first—you NEED to put yourself first. Sure, there will be moments you make sacrifices for others, moments that you go out of your way to help others, and moments that you put others before yourself—that is all great and you should commend yourself on being a genuine person. What you cannot do is beat yourself up for putting yourself first during those other moments. Stop being so hard on yourself, especially for wanting to dedicate your time to YOU. Time on this planet is finite and you have the freedom to spend it however you'd like without explanation to anyone. If you choose to utilize your time for yourself over someone else, then so be it.

People will begin to value your time more when you begin to value it the most yourself. It is during moments of choosing to put yourself first that people will realize how valuable your time actually is—they will begin to appreciate when you sacrifice your time for them.

My daily goal is to run 1.25 miles every day and I preach to others to do the same. While many would think that's random, there is a deeper meaning behind running 1.25 miles every day. The last 0.25 mile symbolizes a lap you once thought you couldn't do—it symbolizes a lap you thought wasn't necessary because you already completed a mile. It's symbolic because you decided not to stop—you pushed forward and gave a little bit more effort. Why? Because you weren't content—you wanted more for yourself. In this life, always continue to push forward. You can't get complacent, ever. Continue to put forth more and more effort. There is so much that you are capable of achieving. Recognize that when you think you are finished, there's actually more work to be done—that there's more opportunity that lies ahead. You should love that—you should be grateful for the opportunity to do more. You should be so eager to do more and accomplish more for yourself. No one likes mediocrity and you shouldn't either. You should be putting all of your effort into the aspects of life that make you happy, and then some. There is no reason that you need to stop—only you can put limits on yourself. You can accomplish as much as you can convince yourself of accomplishing. Whenever you take on a task, you should attack it head-on—you should look to achieve more than what is expected. Personally, I rather be an overachiever than an underachiever. When it comes to the aspects of life that I love and enjoy, I'm going to go all out—I'm going to do so because it only enhances my overall happiness. Remember, when you think you can't do more, you can, and you should.

"Anything in life worth doing is worth overdoing. Moderation is for cowards." — Shane Patton

Go on adventures, book the flight, and see the world—time is finite. There is so much out there to see and experience. The beauty in traveling is the opportunity to meet new people—to experience different cultures and potentially impact the lives you come across. There is so much to learn about yourself and others through travel. If money is your reason for not traveling, remember that you can always make more money—you cannot get back time. Every second you spend contemplating whether you should book the trip is wasted time—just book it. I am here to convince you to spend the money—see the world because you will never have the opportunity to see it again. You don't need to spend copious amounts of money to explore the world around you. You don't need to go on luxurious all-inclusive type trips. There is plenty to see with minimal cost. See what the world has to offer. Get out of your comfort zone and the bubble you are so used to being confined to. Learn about different cultures—try different foods, learn new languages, and engage in activities. Can you imagine living a full life without exploring all that this world has to offer? I can't. As you get older, traveling can become more difficult—so what better time to travel than right now? I hope by the time you get to the next paragraph you will be on a plane to a destination you always wanted to explore.

You don't know everything, you won't know everything, and you don't need to know everything. Stop pressuring yourself to have all the answers. You don't need to have it all figured out. The majority of those you consider successful do not have it all figured out. Life is a daily process—just go with the flow and roll with the punches. Get out there and just go for it. Sometimes the best plan is to not have one at all. Things aren't always going to go your way or as expected. Learn to adapt and overcome whatever is thrown at you. You don't need to have it all figured out to achieve greatness. Be confident in your ability to learn on the fly. Just put forth the effort—put yourself out there constantly. Half the battle is just showing up. You will be amazed at how much you will achieve just by showing up. Do yourself the favor and show up for yourself daily. Prove to yourself that you are capable—you are capable.

Sometimes it's about being at the right place at the right time. So, think about this: what are you doing to set yourself up to be at the right place at the right time? You must do everything in your power to set yourself up for the opportunity in which you seek. You can't rely on luck—you need to rely on hard work. Start putting yourself out there into the world—you will be amazed at how much the world rewards you when you start giving it your all. Being at the right place at the right time requires taking a leap from the place in which you currently are. Take chances—start betting on yourself. Surround yourself with individuals that are driven—that are so hungry for success. Stop thinking that good things are just going to happen to you—go out there and make them happen to you. Put yourself in a position to allow good things to happen to you. You will get nowhere in life relying on getting lucky and if you've convinced yourself that you cannot achieve what you want to because of luck, then you certainly will never be at the right place at the right time. If you have convinced yourself that you have bad luck or that you're unlucky, you will forever remain in the wrong place at the wrong time.

A patient of mine once said, "I feel pain today, but that's okay because it means I'm alive." Think about that phrase for a moment. You are alive and even though today might not be your day, you have the opportunity to make the most of it. You must train yourself to be grateful to be alive even through the toughest of times. You are going to have days of struggle, days of hurt, and days of sorrow, but it could always be worse, and let me tell you, someone out there has it worse. Life isn't perfect—it will never be perfect. You are going to go through moments, days, months, and maybe even years of complete disaster—complete unexplained chaos. While I wish that to never be the case for you, it may happen and it's your mindset that will determine whether or not you let the chaos destroy you. You are strong and you can handle anything that is thrown your way. When life kicks you while you're down, don't just lay there—get up and start kicking back. Nothing good comes out of sulking and feeling sorry for yourself. Doing so does nothing to change the outcome of the situation you are in. Have a positive outlook on life. Tell yourself that when you are at your lowest point, you can always climb higher—that things will get better if you tell yourself that they will. And they will get better, but I can't convince you of that until you convince yourself of it. Be grateful to be alive—be grateful for the life in which you live. Make the most of this life before it is too late.

"Life isn't about waiting for the storm to pass—it's about learning how to dance in the rain."

— Greg Plitt

It's not that negative things are happening to you, it's that you are choosing to look at only the negatives. There is good in everything, I am a firm believer in that, so seek to see the positives. When you feel that negative things just keep happening, it's because you are allowing them to—you are allowing your mind to focus solely on everything going wrong instead of what is going right. Do yourself a favor and create a list of all things positive and negative. Once you have created your list, take a look at what you wrote in the positive column. Your positive list might be shorter than your negative list, but I promise you that once you start focusing on the positives, that list will grow. You will start to see how one positive leads to another—all it takes is one positive to be listed. Remember that life happens—that life isn't always perfect and that life isn't always going to go your way. It's your mindset that determines how you will live your life—whether you will sulk in the negatives or seek the positives. When life isn't going your way, do you sit and think about all that is going wrong or do you put your energy towards all that is going right? Do you focus on the little things that ultimately don't matter or do you focus on ways to create positive action? Stop wasting your time and energy stressing about things that don't matter and events you cannot change. Start looking at the positives in life.

Don't allow people to live rent-free in your head. Don't let the words of others hurt you. Don't let others have the power to bring you down. No one has the power to dictate your life other than you yourself. You are going to come across others that simply don't understand you—that simply do not relate to your cause or what you stand for. You are going to come across others that will not support you and will do everything in their power to bring you down. Do not let them. You cannot waste energy on those who put all of their energy into seeing you fail. You cannot get discouraged by those that don't believe in you. At the end of the day, all that matters is that you believe in yourself. All that matters is that you continue to have a positive impact on those around you, whether others take notice or not. Live this life for you and only you. You are going to have people make comments, question you, put you down, or try to convince you that all you've worked for is a waste of time—just keep moving forward. You are going to have people try to peg you for something you are not—just keep moving forward. You are going to have people try and make you feel worthless—just keep moving forward. That's all you need to do—just keep moving forward. Do not look back—do not stop for anyone.

Move forward in this life—those that want to be a part of your journey will come for the ride I promise you. Don't try and convince others to be a part of your journey—you're wasting your time and energy. Those that truly believe in you won't need any convincing. Those that truly see you for who you are will be there for you through the highs and the lows. Those that understand you and your purpose will be by your side through it all, even when you feel like giving up. Cherish these people—keep them close because they are hard to come by. Cherish them because they will push you to levels you never thought you could reach. Cherish them because, in moments of self-doubt, they will be there to convince you that you are capable of achieving anything you set your mind to. Cherish them because they will be the ones to help propel you forward in this life.

Pay close attention to the ones that don't congratulate you. There are going to be those that are reluctant to congratulate you out of spite, out of jealousy, or because they simply do not want you to succeed. Unfortunately, you might find yourself surrounded by close friends or even loved ones that do not go out of their way to congratulate you. It is in these moments that you should take a step back, reflect, and take note of who truly is a part of your support system. It is in these moments that you will learn who you will move forward in this life with. It is in these moments that you will realize who you have been wasting your energy on all along. Don't forget to acknowledge those that go out of their way to congratulate you—those that go out of their way constantly to check in and see how you are doing. Be grateful for those that congratulate you—those that are truly happy to see you succeed. Pay closer attention to them for they are your support system. Recognize that your support system doesn't just mean family and friends—it means those who sacrifice their own time and energy to lift you up. Your support system doesn't just consist of those close to you. Your support system consists of all individuals that are positive and grateful for you to be a part of their life in some form. Reach out to these people, check in on them, and congratulate them as they congratulate you. Lift up those that make an effort to lift you up.

Takeaway points:

1. There is good in everything—seek to see the positives
2. Don't allow people to live rent-free in your head
3. Just keep moving forward
4. Lift up those that make an effort to lift you up

If multiple people are telling you the same thing about yourself, it might be time to self-reflect. This might be a tough pill to swallow, but you might be the problem. Often, people tend to point fingers elsewhere and fail to acknowledge their wrongdoings. If you notice a trend in how people are acting around you, you either are doing a terrible job at choosing who you are surrounding yourself with or you need to take a closer look at your actions. Many times, it's more than just a coincidence—there is usually some rationale as to why people are acting the way they are around you or towards you. There is no reason to get upset or angry when coming to this realization—it's better to realize and address the issue rather than remain oblivious. It takes a strong individual to admit that they are an issue or that their actions could be better—there is nothing weak about coming to terms with that and admitting it. This is part of self-growth. This is part of how you become a more well-rounded individual and certainly a more likable one. You can't let the opinions others have about you bother you, but that doesn't mean you should neglect them altogether. Unfortunately, sometimes there is some truth to those opinions, and being aware of them can help you grow as an individual. It is better to acknowledge and reflect rather than strictly ignore. You are not going to be liked by everyone, and you shouldn't expect that, but at some point, ask yourself: why is there a trend? This is when you need to turn to those you love and trust—those that you consider a part of your inner circle. These should be the opinions you value the most. Turn to them and simply ask them about your actions. Ask them if you've been a good sibling, a good friend, or a good partner. Sometimes all it takes is asking. Often you won't even realize the effect you are having on those around you. You will never become truly aware unless you ask—it's impossible to make a change if you're not fully aware. You will be surprised by what those you consider close to you have to say—hopefully, it's all positive, but acknowledge the negative and grow from it. Do some self-reflecting and allow yourself to grow as an individual.

Learn to forgive yourself. In this life you are going to make mistakes—you are human. You are not perfect and will never be perfect. You are going to say and do things that you'll later regret. It happens, but what's important is that it doesn't happen again. What's important is that you don't make a habit of making mistakes. You can't continue to beat yourself up over the mistakes you have made. You can't allow the weight of your previous actions to hold you down. Just learn to let go. Allow yourself to heal—to free yourself from any guilt you may have. Remind yourself that you have grown since those actions—that you have reflected and admitted to what you have done wrong. Remind yourself that you did all that you could to remediate the situation and if you didn't, you know that it won't happen again because you won't allow it to. You can't go back and change what you have done—you can only move forward and learn from your mistakes. Apologize to those that you have done wrong. Touch base with those you have hurt—try and mend bridges you have burned. Once you have forgiven yourself, forgive others for the mistakes they have made against you—forgive those that have done you wrong. Don't hold grudges. Learn to see that people can grow and become better versions of themselves. Stop judging people—stop looking at others for who they once were. Look at others for who they are now. People are allowed to make mistakes—it is how people grow. Acknowledge that you could be on either end of it, so learn to forgive—yourself and others. Don't hold on to hate—there is too much love in this world to be shadowed by hate. Holding on to grudges just weighs you down—it prevents you from growing yourself. Grudges prevent you from trusting and loving people. Holding grudges is simply the act of clinching on to negative energy. Let that go—let all of that energy go because you simply do not need it. You have a big heart and there is no room in it for any ounce of negativity.

Forgive yourself.
Forgive others.
Learn to let go.

Pick your battles—some instances aren't worth the energy. Sometimes you have to put your ego aside, swallow your pride, and just move forward. You are going to find yourself in situations where you firmly know you are right, but sometimes proving that you are right just isn't worth it. You shouldn't feel the need to prove to others what you believe in. You shouldn't feel the need to have to defend yourself all of the time. It's okay to walk away. It's okay to ignore conflict for the greater good of both parties. Is proving your point worth it? Is trying to persuade someone of your view on a situation worth the time and energy? I don't know maybe, but more often than not it isn't worth it. When it comes to confrontation, arguing is never the answer—truly nothing good comes out of an argument. If you find yourself in a situation that escalates towards becoming an argument, just walk away. Arguing just sucks the energy out of you—it is mentally draining and does absolutely nothing positive for you. If you find yourself trying to have a civil conversation with someone, but your sole purpose is to prove yourself right instead of remediating the situation, then that's on you—that's a recipe for an argument. You should look to remediate situations if you need to and again if that just isn't working, walk away. Just walk away it's that simple, yet people tend to struggle to do this. People struggle because they cannot swallow their pride—their ego prevents them from doing so. What people need to understand is that being happy triumphs over being right—eliminating arguments or confrontation will certainly lead to more happiness. However, the problem lies in the fact that being right is what makes many people happy. It's a vicious cycle that ultimately leads to dissatisfaction and isolation. People push to prove themselves right, then they prove themselves right, then they become happy, then they're left alone depicted as arrogant and ignorant, and then they're left unhappy only to seek to prove themselves right again. Nobody wants to be around someone who looks to prove themselves right all of the time. Quite frankly, people admire those that can walk away without having to prove that they were right—people admire those that chose happiness over confrontation. If you are someone who feels the need to prove yourself right, next time you are in a confrontation just listen—let the other party do all of the talking and truly just listen. Maybe you'll gain some insight from what they're saying—maybe you'll disagree, but if so, this time just walk away. You must break that cycle of having to be right all of the time and having to prove it to those around you. You do not need to prove anything to anyone but yourself. The need to prove yourself right is only taking away from your ultimate happiness. Pick your battles—watch how much happier you become.

It's okay to pivot and go a different route in life. You are not obligated to stay on the same path. You are free to do whatever you want that makes you happy. In life, you are constantly growing physically, mentally, and spiritually. There might come a time when you have different interests, different passions, and different viewpoints—things change. Change is okay—change is growth. You can't live life unhappy—you can't live life feeling stuck. Just because you spent years in one career doesn't mean you can't change to a completely different one that makes you feel more fulfilled. It is never wasted time when there is something to be learned from it—every day is a lesson. Each day teaches you how to grow, how to be a better person, and how to be happy with yourself. Be happy with yourself and your life—you deserve to be happy. If pivoting and going on a different route in life equates to happiness, then please go for it. Do not wait, do not second guess yourself, and do not fear change. Just go for it—put yourself out there and take the risk. Your happiness is worth the risk, so bet on yourself. Chase all that you want to accomplish and what truly makes you happy. Life is too short to live it for someone else—live your life for you. Don't get complacent with your life—don't just live life content. Live a life that makes you so happy that you become eager to make those around you a part of your journey. Live a life that makes you want to spread your happiness. That is the route in life you should want to take. No matter how many times you need to pivot and go on a different route, just make sure you keep moving forward. Make sure you keep chasing happiness, fulfillment, and pure joy for life itself. Keep moving forward and do not look back. Your happiness is worth the pivot.

"It's okay to pivot in life—your happiness is worth the pivot." — Dr. Tyler Van

Contemplating what you could have done is a waste of time and energy. What you should be doing is allocating that time toward planning your next move. Just like any coach would tell their team to have that next-play mentality, you need to do the same with life. Focus on what you can control right now and what you can do to set yourself up for success. What are you doing at this point in your life that is going to have a positive impact on your future? What have you done today to set yourself up for success tomorrow? You see, maximizing what you do today will only increase your chances of success tomorrow. Furthermore, it will decrease the amount of worry you will have for tomorrow or the future. Putting your energy into what you can control right now will subsequently lead you to better outcomes in the future. Come up with a plan—lay out your next move and what you should be doing right now to enhance your next move. Now, while I think it is beneficial to plan your next move and have that next-play mentality, it becomes detrimental when you plan so far ahead to the point you begin to neglect the present. Do not neglect the present—still live in the moment and do all that you can today to set yourself up for success tomorrow. You don't need to think so far ahead—that is when worrying ensues. Don't worry—be prepared. It is important to know the difference between the two. Worrying about tomorrow or the future is failing to admit to yourself that you did or did not do everything in your power to set yourself up for a positive outcome. If you admit to yourself that you did all that you could do, then you shouldn't be worried. If you admit to yourself that you DID NOT do all that you could do, you still shouldn't worry but recognize that moving forward you need to be more prepared. Being prepared is admitting to yourself that you did all that you could do to set yourself up for a positive outcome and you are ready to take on whatever that outcome may be.

"By failing to prepare, you are preparing to fail."
— Benjamin Franklin

Be genuine—just be a good person it's that simple. Do right by others—lift up those that are around you. You should want to see those around you win. Life is better when everyone is winning. It's tough to grasp that we live in a world where people struggle to be nice to one another. Reach out to someone—tell them that they are doing great and that you are proud of what they are accomplishing. You don't realize how much small gestures like that mean to someone. You don't realize how a small gesture like that can completely turn someone else's day around. Strive to be the reason why someone else had a good day because when you do so, you will have a good day. There is nothing wrong with doing right by others because it makes you feel good. There is no reason to feel guilty about helping others because it makes you feel good—in my mind, that's a win for everyone. If your reason for helping others is because it makes you feel good, then I say go for it—being selfish in that regard is the best type of selfishness.

Take the time to reach out to someone's boss and let them know they are doing a great job. Take the time to compliment someone regarding their extraordinary customer service. Take the time to let someone know that their time in helping you is greatly appreciated. Time is valuable. When someone gives up their time to help you, see the true value in that. Sometimes people just need a little recognition. Sometimes people just need a little reassurance that what they are doing is helpful. Sometimes people just need to be told that they are worthy—that they are completely capable of performing the task at hand. Be that person to reassure others. Whether it's a colleague, teammate, employee, or significant other, it doesn't matter—reassure others that they are doing great. You will be amazed at how much giving someone reassurance can completely change the dynamic of the workplace, competitive team, or any relationship.

In this life, it's important to fight for what's right. Confrontation sucks—no one wants to be in a predicament, but you need to stand up for yourself, for what you believe in, and for others. You can't let others walk all over you. You can't allow yourself to get taken advantage of. Don't let your kindness be taken for weakness. Continue to be strong, continue to be passionate, and continue to fight for the greater good—no matter how big or small. Continue to do right by others—never stoop down to the level of those who try to bring you down. Be kind—you won't get anywhere being argumentative and egotistical. Don't allow yourself to just be a number—let your voice be heard. Give others a reason to remember your name, but let it be for good reasoning. Let it be because you stood up for what you believe in. Let it be because you went out of your way to stick up for others—that you were the voice for others who feared giving any sort of resistance. In society or the workplace, you need to stand up for what you believe in. You also need to realize that with that may come backlash—that you may be put in uncomfortable situations. Understand that sometimes doing what's right isn't easy—that doing what's right can start to isolate you from the majority. Don't forget your ethical code—continue to follow your moral compass. Live a life doing what you believe in because that's truly living.

Go out of your way to help others. Give to the universe and the universe will give back to you. You are going to get what you put in and then some. Always have good intentions. You will be amazed at the results you start to see, regarding any aspect of your life, when you give back first. There is so much in this world to be done—there are so many people that could use your help. Start by just helping out those around you—help out those in your inner circle. Watch how contagious being generous and kind can be. You will start to see those around you win and then you will begin to win—more so than ever before. Next thing you know you're surrounded by winners—a huge network of individuals all seeking to get the most out of this life. It's truly a domino effect—you help others and in return, they help others. There is nothing like helping others—nothing compares to that feeling. To help be the reason someone succeeded, that someone was motivated, or that someone gained a valuable lesson, that's priceless. The energy you experience when you constantly surround yourself with those eager to win is indescribable. Nobody wants to constantly be surrounded by those losing, let's just call it how it is—so why not be the one to help transform that person into a winner? We all have the tools to win. Don't be selfish—share those tools with others. Strive to make the community a better place. Strive to make those around you happier, motivated, and successful. Provide those around you with the knowledge that was bestowed upon you. Help guide others to live a more positive lifestyle. Help those struggling to find their way—be the one to direct them. Someone needs to step up and be a helping hand—that person needs to be you because you can do so. Try and go out of your way to help someone today.

The world isn't out to get you. Stop thinking about the worst in every situation. Stop resorting to thinking that everyone has this ulterior motive and that their agenda is to make your life miserable—to be difficult for the sole purpose of giving you a hard time. Start recognizing that there is more good in this world than you think. Not everyone is your enemy—not everyone wants to see you fail. In fact, people want to see you succeed—people want you to accomplish your goals. People believe in you—you inspire others. You, whether you believe it or not, have made an impact on those around you. People are watching you—whether it be from the front row or from afar. People are noticing—people are paying attention. While you might get some chirps here and there from the crowd, people are talking—people are seeing what you're accomplishing. Sure, there will be negativity said about you, but just know the positivity that is being said outweighs such negativity. The world can be a dark place, but the light always shines through—good always prevails. There's more good in this world than bad—trust that. Your mind needs to always resort to the good—stop thinking about the bad. Stop thinking about the negativity that is being said about you because it doesn't matter. People can only bring you down if you let them—don't allow someone to have that power. You don't need to be so defensive all the time—you don't need to be on high alert. Learn to let your guard down—learn to put your trust in others. It can be difficult, but you need to try. People want to support you, people want to help you, and people want to lift you up—that can only happen if you let them. Learn to open your heart up to the world because some want to open theirs up to you. Start trusting that the world can be a good place.

The world isn't out to get you.

I want you to try this—it may change your perspective forever. Raise your hand as high as you can. Now raise it just a little bit higher. Now I ask you, were you able to raise your hand higher? If so, why didn't you raise your hand as high as you could the first time? This was an exercise that was shown to me at a very young age and a lesson that has stuck with me ever since. Often, people save their energy for the right moment or the perfect opportunity. Unfortunately, the right moment or the perfect opportunity does not exist. You should be putting all of your energy into what you want to accomplish right now because the opportunity is right now. Many individuals sit around waiting and waiting for the right opportunity to arise—time just passes by as they fail to realize that the opportunity is right now. You should be giving it your all, day in and day out. With any task that is given to you, your approach should be with 100% effort. You should look to capitalize on any opportunity that is thrown your way. Go out there and create opportunities for yourself. Whether you're on the field or in the workplace, the same concept applies. Stop waiting around. Stop saving your energy for the right moment. You know there is so much you want to accomplish, so why aren't you going out there and doing it? There is always going to be uncertainty—the destination or the outcome may be unknown. That shouldn't stop you from doing what you want to accomplish. You need to try and you need to try with all of your effort. You will never know unless you try and you will never get to where you want to be unless you put everything you have into succeeding. Put all of your being into everything that you do and watch your life transform—you know you are capable of doing so. Be smart and be methodical, but remember the perfect opportunity does not exist. At what point does being smart and methodical become just wasted time? Something to think about.

"Are you willing to sprint when the distance is unknown?" — Lewis Caralla

Next time you wake up, take a moment to think about the opportunity you have before you. You have the opportunity to be great—the opportunity to do anything you desire. You can do what many others cannot—be grateful for that. Make the most of today and every day. Take control of your day—dictate the outcome of your day. Don't just sit there and let time pass—make the most of every second. Capitalize on every opportunity that comes your way, no matter how big or small. You are the author of your story—no one else has the power to write your narrative. Start writing your story—start creating opportunities for yourself. Don't be someone who just goes through the motions, for that is not living. Shake things up, stand out, and create some waves—be positively disruptive. Let the world know who you are and what you stand for. Let those around you know that you are here to make a positive impact—that you are here on this planet to leave your mark. Attack every day like it's your last—let your actions do the talking. Wake up, be grateful for the opportunity, and make the most of your day.

"Either you run the day or the day runs you."
— Jim Rohn

People struggle every day—people fight a daily battle. If you're one of those people, just know you're not alone. It's okay to ask for help—you shouldn't feel like a burden. People want to help you—people want you to do well and be well. Don't give up—giving up is easy and you were built to get through tough times. You were built to withstand life's challenges. You were built to overcome every obstacle. Don't give up. Embrace the struggle—embrace it with open arms and then conquer it. Take control of your life and just keep going. No matter how hard it can be just keep going. If you need help on your journey, reach out to someone. Do not be afraid to ask for help and guidance. People are there for you—people are there to help you take control of your life. People are there to help you fight your battle and win. You are a winner. There's no reason for you to have to fight your battle alone. You don't need to prove anything to anyone. Asking for help doesn't make you weak. Asking for help doesn't make you less of a person. Asking for help makes you smart—it makes you responsible. Asking for help is taking ownership—it is acknowledging that there is a problem and you are putting forth effort to fix it. Asking for help is making an effort to become the best version of you. Just ask for help. If you know someone who needs help, reach out and offer it. Take the initiative to help someone be better. Take into account that someone may be struggling to ask for help as they fear it makes them less—reassure them that it does not. Check in on those that you think may be struggling. We are all in this together.

You're going to have days that the universe tests you—days you just feel like giving up. You're going to have days you feel angry, upset, and frustrated—days you feel like your inner soul is screaming because you feel like you can't catch a break. Just go back to the drawing board and remember your recipe for no bad days. Remember how far you've come to maintain a positive mindset—to not let any external factors affect your inner peace. Remember that in the end, it all works out and that it can always be worse. You can't let inconveniences or "setbacks" determine your mood. I put "setbacks" in quotes because a setback only exists if you let it exist. If you treat every obstacle as a lesson, did you really get set back? Or did you learn from the situation and move forward in a positive light? What you may consider as a setback can be an opportunity to propel forward—to grow as an individual. You see, it all depends on your perspective and how you choose to view each situation you are put in. You have the power to determine your mood and only you should have that power. When the universe tests you, there are two options—to fold or stand tall. Sure, it might not be easy to stand tall, but you need to try. You can't fold—you can never fold.

Takeaway points:

1. Remember your recipe for no bad days
2. Don't let external factors affect your inner peace
3. A setback only exists if you let it exist

Stop being so hasty. You don't need to solve all of your problems right this second. Take a deep breath and process what is happening. It's all going to work out. You don't need to get worked up over the obstacles you face in life. You are going to be tasked with solving issues and when you come across such issues, take a moment to reflect. Take a moment to prioritize all that needs to be accomplished in your life. You are not going to solve all issues, those that are personal or in the workplace, at once, and you shouldn't expect yourself to do just that. It will all get done because you know deep down you will get it done, so stop worrying. Too often we allow ourselves to get flustered, overwhelmed, and frustrated primarily because we expect so much out of ourselves. We also expect life to be one easy ride and it just isn't, plain and simple. Stop being so hard on yourself and give yourself some credit—you are doing a great job. Next time you are faced with a problem, just take a deep breath. Is there a solution to the problem? If yes, good stop worrying. If not, good stop worrying. Sometimes, all it takes is taking a deep breath and taking a step back to reflect on what is actually happening. If you are faced with an issue that is time sensitive, just know that no good result will come out of you rushing to get it done without a plan—without truly processing what is going on. This need, or this urge, to fix all problems all at once is a habit you must break—you are going to drive yourself crazy. Learn to prioritize, and quite frankly, learn when to not get involved in issues that do not need your solving. Sometimes, it is truly not your problem. Sometimes, you should just delegate or refer to someone else who can better solve the issue. Acknowledge that you have plenty of your own problems or tasks that need attending—there's no need to take on those of others. There's a reason in healthcare specialties exist. Not only does it allow for better quality care, but it can't be expected of a single practitioner to be able to solve all issues or know everything at that. So, the next time you feel like you are being hasty, take a deep breath, take a step back, and simply process what is happening.

Takeaway points:

1. Stop being hasty
2. Take a deep breath and process what is happening
3. Prioritize
4. Learn to delegate or refer to someone else who can better solve the issue

Learn to be patient—eliminate “I can’t wait” from your vocabulary. While “I can’t wait” is a common phrase, take a moment to realize what you are actually saying. You are literally saying that you are incapable of waiting for a certain moment. You are implying that you are struggling to enjoy the moment right now. You are implying that you are so fixated on the future, that you are disregarding the present. Enjoy your time right now—enjoy the process. You can wait and to be honest, sometimes you are going to have to do just that. By saying “I can’t wait,” you are conditioning your mind to get anxious—you are conditioning your mind to have this anticipation for something that has not happened yet. Now let me ask you this, what if it doesn’t happen? What if all that you couldn’t wait for just falls through? Pretty disappointing right? What is even more disappointing is that you spent all of your time anxious for something so far in the future, rather than being present in the moment. Listen, I am not saying to stop looking forward to future endeavors, but what I am saying is that often doing so creates pent-up anxiety. Go ahead and look forward to the future, but don't disregard all that is happening in your life at this very moment. Time is precious. Time is a valuable asset, so enjoy that asset—enjoy it because you cannot get it back. "I can't wait though"—well the thing is you can and you're going to have to. Stop creating a portal for unwarranted and unnecessary anxiety—you do just that when you fail to live in the moment and proceed to live in the future. Do yourself the favor and eliminate "I can't wait" from your vocabulary.

You have a big heart and it's good that you care, but sometimes it is necessary to stop caring so much. Sometimes you just need to care less and live carefree. Learn to not get so fixated on certain aspects of your life. It's okay to let things be—to let life just play out. Sometimes you truly just need to let go—to move on. Don't stop being passionate, don't stop loving, and certainly don't stop caring, but learn to acknowledge when caring so much affects your well-being. Oftentimes, caring so much leads to overthinking, hurt, and disappointment.

When that tends to occur, it's usually because you're caring too much about things that do not warrant it—things that do not matter in the grand scheme of it all. Learn to recognize when you are caring too much about the aspects of your life that do not warrant it.

Identify those that you put your heart and soul into—that you devote time and energy towards. Acknowledge those that you care so much about and think, is it reciprocated? The amount of caring you put into that individual, is it reciprocated even in the slightest? Determine whether or not that individual deserves your time and energy. You shouldn't help someone with the intention of it being reciprocated, that's not how you should live life, but recognize when you are constantly doing for others that would never do for you. Your time is valuable—your energy is valuable. There will come a time in your life when you finally realize that—maybe that time is right now. Apply this to the workplace—are you valued at work or are you viewed as just a number? Do your efforts get acknowledged? Does the difference you are making get recognition? Again, do not work hard with the intent of seeking praise, that is not the point, but value your time and energy. Don't be just a number—you have worked way too hard to be known as that. You are motivated, you are knowledgeable, and you are caring—you deserve to be known and receive the energy back that you put towards others, regarding all aspects of life. Acknowledge all of those that put their time and energy into you—thank them and appreciate them, because their time and energy is valuable.

You are going to have days when you are stressed and you let your emotions get the best of you. You are going to have days that test your growth. You are going to have days that you could have handled better, but you didn't. You are going to have days when you feel upset with yourself, but you cannot sulk. You cannot dwell on what you could have done better—that time is gone. Move on and focus on what is next—the time that has passed is not worth being upset over. You are going to have days when you feel anxious, overwhelmed, and frustrated. Do not let anxiety win. Do not let stress win. Do not let anything that affects you negatively win. Do not succumb to the person you once were. You are mentally tough—you are capable of getting through anything that life throws at you. You have grown so much—you cannot allow yourself to take steps back. Realize that life will be chaotic sometimes. The question becomes, how well are you able to perform in chaos? How well are you able to handle life's challenges? Embrace it all. Accept life's challenges with open arms. You cannot let your emotions win. You are in control and you must remain in control.

Teach yourself to see the positive in everything. Your life will change when you start to see the positive in everything. For example, do you find yourself feeling anxious? Instead of viewing anxiety as a burden, view such anxiety as a driving force to make you work harder. Maybe such anxiety will be your reason to stay busy because being busy calms your mind. Constantly flip the script in life and convince yourself that you are always ahead. Convince yourself that anytime life goes wrong, it's actually for the right reasons. You can't lose if you are constantly optimistic. What is meant to be will be. There is no reason to force an outcome—if something isn't happening the way you'd like it to, it's probably for a good reason and you need to convince yourself of that. Convince yourself that it's all part of the plan. Everything truly happens for a reason, so start seeing the positives in that reason. Whatever life throws at you, use it to grow, and use it to your advantage. Turn an unfavorable outcome into a favorable one—there is always a way if you believe there is. That's the beauty of seeing the world in a positive light—nothing will be able to bring you down. Watch how much mentally tougher you become when you view the world and all of its misfortunes positively. Watch how happier you become when you start to see the positive in everything.

Stop with the "I can't catch a break mentality." That mentality is exhausting—it does nothing but bring you down and those around you down with you. No one wants to hear it. Truly, no one wants to listen to how miserable your life is because "you can't catch a break." Life's tough and everyone has problems—everyone has tribulations they are trying to deal with. You aren't unlucky, you are simply dealing with life. What would life be without problems? What would life be without obstacles, challenges, and tough decisions? There would be no growth in life if it was easy. Learn to adapt—learn that when things go south you have to buckle down and figure it out. Sitting there saying to yourself "I can't catch a break" does absolutely nothing—no issue in life is solved with that mentality. Moping and pouting about an issue do nothing to benefit you—you are just wasting time and energy. Complaining to others about your problems does nothing but bring them down with you—who would want to be around that? Would you want to be around those constantly complaining? Or would you rather surround yourself with those that are motivated to attack life head-on? I know my answer. Negativity just sucks the life out of you and the life out of those around you. You should strive to motivate and lift people up, not bring them down. Do yourself the favor and eliminate the phrase "I can't catch a break" from your mind—do not think it, do not speak it, and do not live it.

Stop comparing yourself to others. The only person you should be comparing yourself to is who you were yesterday. Your life will never be like anyone else's—your journey will never be like anyone else's. You can't get discouraged when someone else, who put in less work than you, achieves greater results—it happens. What you really should take note of is that you're even aware of how much work someone else is putting in. Why are you dedicating your energy to someone else's journey? Why are you so invested in what other people are achieving? Start dedicating that energy to yourself—start becoming more invested in what you can be achieving. Focus on yourself—focus on what you can be doing in this very moment to take your life to new heights. Do not get discouraged if those around you are at different points in their lives than you—do not get discouraged if those around you are achieving more than you. There is no rule book to life—there isn't a set time frame for when things need to happen. Your life is unique and cannot be compared to the lives of others. When and how you accomplish tasks will never be identical to that of others. You will never know what someone is truly going through, so what you're comparing yourself to is just surface level anyway—just stop. You will find yourself unhappy if you continue to compare yourself to others.

Don't ever be embarrassed—own it. Stop making excuses—own it. Stop worrying about what other people think and just own it. You are going to make mistakes, you are going to embarrass yourself, and you are going to fail miserably—instead of rationalizing as to why, just own it and move on. Have some confidence in yourself and bounce back. There is no reason to care so much about what other people think of you—you aren't living your life to please others. People tend to make excuses, rationalize decisions made, and feel embarrassed because they value the opinion of others way too highly. People also do this because they begin to value their self-image way more than who they actually are. Own who you are—let the world see that version of you. Let the world continue to see your authentic self. Live for the embarrassing moments—live for the moments of failure because it is how you handle those moments that make life fun. How you handle those moments is what others value—no one wants to hear excuses. Own it and show the world how your authentic self handles a situation that is not ideal. That is what is truly inspiring to others—the ability to take any situation and handle it with grace, regardless of the outcome. The next time you feel embarrassed, just laugh and move on. The next time you fail miserably, acknowledge the failure and move on. Learn from it, own it, and stop making excuses. No one cares—seriously, no one cares. The reality is, you are so concerned with what other people think of you while they're not giving you and your actions much thought. It's not that deep—people aren't sitting there dissecting and analyzing your every move. If so, then those people aren't spending their time focusing on bettering themselves—that should be enough to convince you to not be so concerned with what others think.

Just focus on yourself and own it.

Be at peace with your past—recognize that who you once were is not who you are now. Lessons were learned, changes were made, and growth ensued. You cannot allow yourself to dwell on your past. You cannot allow yourself to get upset over the choices that you made. The past is the past and as cliché as that sounds, that is truly what it is. Focus on who you are right now and put all of your energy into improving that version of yourself. The past happened for a reason—you would not be who you are today if it weren't for your past. Instead of letting the past upset you, you should be thankful for it. No matter how terrible your past may be, it led you to grow into the individual you are right now. The path to getting to where you are right now may not have been easy, but you made it. You made it and you became smarter, stronger, and happier along the way. Without your past, you wouldn't be you—you wouldn't be this amazing individual that is accomplishing so much. Do not let your past haunt you—do not let your past determine who you are right now. Acknowledge your past and be at peace with it because without your past there is no future.

What you are doing, what you are accomplishing for yourself, is helping others and you don't even know it. You don't even realize the impact you are having on those around you. It may be thousands of individuals or it may be just one person, but if you could help just one person, one soul, then it is worth it. Realize that impacting one life will compound over time to many. People are taking notice of what you are doing. People are seeing what you are trying to achieve and trust me they love it. They are buckled in for the ride and they stand behind you. Remember, when you are doubting yourself, you have individuals around you that are believing in you. You are surrounded by individuals that stand behind your message. It is in those moments of self-doubt that you need to keep going. You cannot give up—for yourself and for them. You may not get the recognition you deserve, but that's not why you started doing it in the first place. It's not about the recognition. It's not about the publicity. It's not about the praise. It's about doing what makes you happy. It's about bringing yourself joy with the potential of inspiring others to feel the same way. It's about motivating yourself to be your best self and if that inspires just one person to do the same, then what a bonus that is. Your actions should not be dictated by the purpose of seeking acknowledgment from those around you. Keep doing it for yourself. People are going to take notice whether they believe in you or not—that won't change, so just do it for yourself. Do not lose sight of your purpose—to be better for yourself with potentially inspiring others to do the same. You cannot help others unless you help yourself first. That phrase is one that you seriously need to drill deep into your mind.

So, while you continue to aspire to inspire, let it happen naturally—do not force it. Do not force it because you'll begin to lose grasp on why you began the process in the first place—for you. I know you're eager to help others and make a difference, but let it happen organically. Let the opportunity to do those things unfold. You already initiated the opportunity when you started striving to be the best version of yourself. You created this opportunity you seek without even realizing it, so start trusting the process. Your voice will be heard. Your time will come and your voice will be heard—if it hasn't been heard already. You just need to be patient—keep doing what you're doing and be patient. You should seek to help others, but remember why you are doing so. Do you want to help others because it makes you happy or do you want to help others because you crave attention? I hope it's because you genuinely enjoy helping others and it makes you happy. Do not force what you are trying to achieve in this life—there is no reason to force it. It is going to happen if you just allow it to happen. Appreciate the fact that you can make a difference without even realizing you are doing so. Appreciate the fact that your voice can be heard without even speaking. Realize that you're waiting for your moment to come, to help others and make a difference, but that moment has already occurred and is occurring.

Takeaway points:

1. If you can help just one person in the process, then your process was worth it
2. Do not do it for recognition, publicity, or praise
3. Allow inspiring others to happen naturally by simply living your life with the best intentions
    a. Example: Go to the gym at 5:00 AM because it makes you happy, not because you are trying to inspire others to do the same. It all comes down to your intentions.

I can confidently say I am good at helping others. I preach going out of your way to help others—I practice going out of my way to help others. However, one of the toughest realizations I had to come to terms with was that even though I was good at helping others, I found myself struggling to help myself. There were times I struggled to take my own advice. I've mentioned this before—I was always good at being positive for others, yet I found it difficult at times to be positive for myself. So, I am here to tell you to start taking your own advice. Start putting all of the principles you preach to practice—especially for yourself. If you don't practice what you preach to the fullest, you are doing a disservice to yourself. You may be great at influencing others to live life to their utmost potential, but what good is that if you can't convince yourself to do the same? I think I became so good at helping others and being positive for others because I knew what it felt like to be on the opposite side of the spectrum—I didn't want others to feel the way I felt. I didn't want others to feel frustrated, have self-doubt, be worried, or be stressed—I never wanted anyone to experience those negative emotions. I convinced myself that as long as others didn't feel the way I felt, then I succeeded. If someone was feeling weak, I was always there to be strong for them—yet when I felt weak, I failed to be strong for myself. It's a crazy concept to grasp, I get it, even I have a tough time understanding it and I still try to make sense of it all. What I do know is that you need to step up for yourself. You don't need to go through battles alone, but you need to try and step up for yourself. Just think about how much better life would be if you just listened to yourself—if you took your own advice more often. You have seen the impact your advice has had on others. You know what works and what doesn't work—so live out your own advice. You deserve to be as happy as those you have made around you. You deserve to feel as strong and as motivated as those you have made around you. You will help others, even more, when you help yourself first. By being better for yourself, you are ultimately being better for others—so if you want to have the greatest impact on those around you, you'll have to have the greatest impact on yourself first. Do yourself a favor and take your own advice.

Practice what you preach—a common saying that holds such value.

Invest in yourself. You can't put a price tag on your health. You can't put a price tag on your well-being. You can't put a price tag on your future. Go all in on yourself—you only get one life, so start taking care of it. You shouldn't stress about money when it comes to your health, your well-being, or your future. Health is wealth—do all that you can to take care of yourself and maximize your time spent on this planet. Invest in whatever makes you happy. Whether it's time or money, invest it towards aspects of life that bring you joy. Your future is valuable and all that you are doing at this very moment is contributing to it. Buy books, sign up for seminars, go to a workshop or retreat, hire a health coach, join a gym, etc.—the list of assets that can, and will, benefit your life goes on. These are the type of resources that you should never regret spending money on. Such resources will impact your life—they will provide valuable lessons that you will utilize for the rest of your life. What is even better is that many of the resources named can be acquired for free—just because something is more expensive does not mean it is more valuable. Some of the best books that can transform your life, and I mean truly shift your life in a positive direction, come at little to no cost. Just invest in yourself—stop second-guessing it or feeling guilty about doing so. You are important—you yourself are your most important asset. Nothing in this life is more important than your health, your well-being, and your future. That may seem selfish, that may seem arrogant, but it's true. The quicker you realize that it's okay to invest in yourself first, the more of an impact you'll have on those around you. If you want to make a difference, if you want to create change, or if you want to create opportunities for others, invest in yourself first. It's important that you start investing in yourself and there's no better time to start than right now.

Make time for yourself. Yeah, it's important to work hard and to help others, but when was the last time you truly made time for yourself? Start prioritizing yourself more. Start realizing that there is so much more to life than just work. Also realize that it's okay to be alone—that it's normal to enjoy time with yourself. Sometimes you need just that—time alone. Time alone to self-reflect and to truly relax is crucial to your mental well-being. You can't keep neglecting your well-being for the sake of others. Start allocating time for what truly makes you happy and then prioritize that time. Listen, we all have obligations, but taking care of ourselves should be at the top of the list. There is a finite amount of time that we as human beings will get to spend on this planet. When you begin to break down that time, it becomes eye-opening—just think that 2/3 of the day is spent working and sleeping. The remaining 8 hours usually involve daily tasks that cannot be neglected, so within those 8 hours, you begin to slowly diminish the amount of time spent on yourself. So, of the 168 hours in a week, you're looking at less than 56 hours spent on yourself doing what you truly want to be doing. Life does not have to be this way—it shouldn't be this way. You can maximize those 8 hours if you simply prioritize and make taking care of yourself important. You cannot neglect yourself—you cannot go through life not maximizing those 8 hours. Hopefully, you get more than 8 hours. It's all possible if you make it possible. You just need to start putting yourself first. Take a vacation—go see the world. Time is valuable. YOUR time is valuable—so start making time for yourself.

What is your non-negotiable? What is that one thing that must be done every single day no matter what? For me, it's movement—I need to move my body one way or another every single day. Whether it's a strenuous workout or a brisk walk, my body is moving—no negotiating. I have a few non-negotiables, but movement is by far at the top of the list. Movement is medicine—the power of movement is so beneficial to one's health and should be on everyone's list of non-negotiables. Prioritize what is truly important to you and implement it into your daily regimen consistently. Be disciplined enough to not have that inner contemplation of whether or not something is going to get done. Whatever you decide is important to you needs to become a non-negotiable. You will notice a dramatic change in your attitude, your spirit, and your work ethic when you consistently complete your non-negotiable daily. There will come a time when your non-negotiable is engrained so deep into your daily routine that it becomes second nature—it becomes a habit. That's the goal. You should strive for your non-negotiable to become a habit, to the point you no longer give it any thought—you just get up and do it. When you get to the point of absolutely no contemplation with yourself, none whatsoever, that is when you know your non-negotiable has transformed from a task to a habit. The obvious rationale here is that doing something beneficial, consistently every day, is going to positively impact your life in many ways. Your non-negotiable may have physical benefits, it may have mental benefits, or it may have spiritual benefits, but the common denominator to every non-negotiable is the sense of pride it brings you. The feeling of being productive, consistently, will directly affect your well-being. For me, I consistently implement movement into my daily regimen every single day to the point that I cannot visualize a day without it. I prefer *starting* my day with some form of movement. Unfortunately, when life happens and I cannot *start* my day with movement, I see a dramatic shift in how my day goes. If the timing of when I perform some type of movement directly impacts my mood, my motivation, my spirit, and my work ethic, just imagine a day without it—I can't. The point I am trying to make is that you will see how your non-negotiable plays a role in how your day goes—you will see how this habit directly correlates to your progress in life.

Every day should feel like it's almost Friday. You should never dread your day. You should look forward to each day. People tend to dread Monday—you should embrace Monday. It's such a bizarre concept that we go through life so eager to enjoy two out of seven days a week. Why does it take a weekend to make your week feel worthy? Why is it that we look forward to only 48 hours each week? People need to start looking forward to each day with the same anticipation they have for the weekend. So many individuals would be significantly happier if they approached each day like it was a Saturday. It's all just your mindset—it all comes down to how you perceive your day-to-day life. Instead of dreading Monday and the start of your work week, be grateful for the opportunity you have in front of you. Be grateful for the ability to do whatever it is that you do. Be grateful to have a job. If you simply hate your job, get a new job—let's not overcomplicate things here. Your happiness means more than anything. I know what you're thinking, that statement is insensitive—that some people need to work a job they may not enjoy to provide for their loved ones. If that's the case, then a matter of changing one's mindset is even more pertinent here. If you start approaching each day, convinced that you will have a great day regardless of the circumstances, then you will have a great day. Your mindset is so powerful—how you think your day will go will ultimately determine how your day will be. If you think you are going to have a terrible day, a terrible week, or a terrible year, well buckle up because you're in for a long ride. You should be thoroughly excited every time you wake up. You should feel eager to attack the day. You should genuinely enjoy completing tasks—there's nothing like having a list and the satisfaction of crossing a task off that list. You should be filled with happiness and gratitude every single day, regardless of what day it is. When you start looking forward to the weekend, week after week, your life will begin to speed up. You won't even realize it—you will forget to live in the now. Looking forward to each weekend turns into looking forward to a vacation, which turns into looking forward to retirement. Next thing you know, you're old asking yourself where did life go and how did I get to this point? And I'm here to tell you that you will get to that point if you constantly look forward to the moments that you are not present in. You will get to that point if you dread each day and look forward to only two out of the seven days a week. I've heard so many individuals say, "The older you get, the faster time goes." Well, I think the main contributor to that is that people spend so much time anticipating future moments—that people wait for future moments to come instead of maximizing the moments that are happening right now. I think as people get older, they start to contemplate if they should have done things differently—so they spend their current time anxious or stressed about moments they cannot change because they've convinced themselves it is too late. This ultimately just wastes more time and makes time feel faster. Just live in the now. Be present in the moment and don't dread each day—live for each day. Anticipating the future or contemplating the past will only speed up time—the finite time that we each have on this planet. You don't want to look back and question where the time went—you are going to want to look back knowing that you lived in the moment day in and day out because you were truly grateful for each day.

Don't feed into the aspects of life that make you unhappy—avoid negativity at all costs. You cannot allow negativity to grow inside of you simply because you fed into it. The second you begin to feed into any ounce of negativity is the second you begin to set yourself up for failure. It will be at that moment that you initiate a decline in your well-being. You may not notice it at that moment, but feeding into negativity will slowly compound over time. Feed into the aspects of life that make you happy and let that compound over time. Your overall happiness is determined by what you feed your mind—what you feed your mind will dictate your overall well-being. You essentially become what you surround yourself with—you become what you decide to absorb on a daily basis. How you speak, what you read, what you watch on television, your job, and who you spend your time with socially, are just a few of the many factors that contribute to your level of happiness. Many don't even realize that speaking negatively about others or a situation directly affects them. When you speak negatively, and it becomes a constant occurrence, you train your mind to see the negatives first before noticing the positives—this is regarding any aspect of life. By far the worst thing you can do is talk negatively about yourself as you will begin to only notice what is "wrong" with you rather than acknowledging all of your accomplishments—nothing is wrong with you, so stop trying to convince yourself that there is. Take note of the environment you continuously put yourself in and have a deep conversation with yourself if such an environment is conducive to your well-being. Does the environment you find yourself in daily feed into positivity or negativity? If it's the latter, get yourself out of that environment. Just your presence amongst negativity is enough to affect your well-being, even if you feel you are doing your best to avoid it. Just listening to negativity amongst others is enough to take a toll on your overall happiness. Start feeding into the aspects of life that provide you with growth, knowledge, and overall happiness.

Be a team player. Do whatever it takes to win. You might be placed into a role that you don't necessarily agree with, whether on the field or in the workplace, but you should do everything in your power to excel at that role. Perform at your highest level always. Whatever is asked of you, demonstrate that you can contribute significantly. No role is beneath you, so check your ego. Be versatile—be open-minded. More importantly—be motivated. Be motivated to prove to yourself that you can perform outside of your comfort zone. Be motivated to be that person, or that reason, that your team thrives. Performing in a role that is unconventional to you is only going to provide you with skills that will further enhance your ability to succeed in life. When tasks are asked of you that technically aren't in your "job description," instead of complaining, you should jump right on it. You should take it as another opportunity to grow your skillset. You should take it as an opportunity to prove to yourself that you can literally do anything and you can do anything very well. Have this mindset so that whenever you are asked to perform, you are ready to perform at the highest level. You will begin to realize how much easier it is to perform at a high level, especially when put on the spot or given a task at short notice, when you've conditioned yourself to perform any task with a high level of intensity. As ridiculous as that may sound, when you've become accustomed to performing daily tasks with a high level of intensity, the less difficult any new task will be. The more outside of your comfort zone you allow yourself to be, the more skills you will acquire, and the easier it will be to be a team player regardless of the team you are on. You should ask yourself, "If I was thrown into this profession, how well would I perform?" or "If I was put on this athletic team, how well would I contribute?" Now, regardless of your current profession or if you're an athlete, the answer should be, "I would perform and contribute well." The reason is, work ethic is half the battle—sure knowledge and skill go a long way, but how hard you are willing to work and learn goes even further. You should realize that having a great work ethic, even without having all of the knowledge and skills required to perform a task, an occupation, or a sport, is going to allow you to contribute in some way. Wanting to be a team player and having that eagerness to help will allow you to strive in any position you are put in. You should be thoroughly convinced that if you were asked to perform a role completely unrelated to your current job or sport, you would find a way to make a difference—that you would find a way to allow that team to succeed because, at the end of the day, no task is too big or too small for you. Nothing is beneath you—you are going to do whatever it takes to add value to any team you are put on. The moment you begin to realize that you can adapt to any role and that you can be a true team player is the moment you begin to win the greatest game of all—the game of life.

Takeaway points:

1. Be a team player
2. Be versatile
3. Be motivated
4. Perform any task with a high level of intensity

I have always preached, and continue to preach, that individuals should put all of their energy into everything that they do. Someone once asked me, "Shouldn't you conserve your energy?" While my immediate response was to say no, I stopped and thought for a second—it made me think deeper than the concept of just "giving it your all." So, I asked to elaborate, and that individual said, "Well, shouldn't you want to produce the most by utilizing the least amount of your time and energy?" I immediately began to think of machinery or equipment—the ones that are considered the best are the ones that utilize the least amount of energy to yield a maximum amount of output quickly. That machinery or equipment would, by definition, be considered optimal and efficient. It made me think, why don't we apply that concept to life? While I still think individuals need to give it their all with anything that they want to achieve in life, I need to preface that we can't neglect to be efficient. Giving maximum effort into anything that you do is important, but being efficient is just as important as well. Work smarter not harder, right? We all have heard that saying before. While I believe that statement stands true, I also believe it can be a trap for not putting forth any hard work at all. Don't let being efficient get confused with being lazy. Obtaining the most in life while putting forth the least amount of energy may be a goal of yours—some want to make a lot of money while doing the least amount of work. I'm not saying that isn't possible, of course it's possible, I just think the fastest way in getting to that specific goal isn't by conserving energy. I think those that make the most by doing the least didn't get to that point in their life by not giving it their all first—I don't think they got to that stage in their life by conserving energy. There is a fine line between not doing enough and doing too much. I also think society, as a whole, tends to fall on the "not doing enough" side of the spectrum. I personally rather give it my all and do too much than come up short by not doing enough. People tend to not do enough because they were overly concerned with working smarter, not harder. The point I'm trying to make is that you should continue to put all of your energy into everything that you do because I firmly believe you will increase your chances of achieving your goals that way. Yet, you can't neglect to be efficient in what you do. Why not try working smarter AND harder? Something to think about.

Do you find yourself constantly seeking reassurance? Start trusting the fact that everything happening to you is meant to happen to you. Start trusting the fact that everyone in your life is meant to be in your life. Fight the constant urge to be validated and reassured regarding every aspect of your life—it's exhausting. Not only is it exhausting, but it's also the fastest way to find yourself isolated from the world. Many that seek reassurance find themselves pushing people away—they push people out of their lives with the hope that the ones they pushed away will fight to come back. You shouldn't feel that you need to push people away to determine if they are meant to be there in the first place. If they weren't meant to be in your life, then they wouldn't be. Stop second-guessing opportunities that cross your path—just go for it. You don't need the reassurance that it's going to work out—just find out. If it doesn't work out, then there's your answer. What's the fun in being reassured that it's worth it before even finding out for yourself? Don't you want to enjoy the journey? Don't you want to enjoy the uncertainties? A little turbulence here and there never hurt anyone—it doesn't have to be smooth sailing all of the time and it won't be. You will find yourself spending way too much time seeking reassurance that you will miss the opportunity to learn, grow, and simply experience what life has to offer. Come to terms with the fact that it's okay to be scared. Being scared only means you are uncertain—being uncertain means you get the opportunity to learn and grow. If you constantly receive reassurance from others that it's going to work out, man are you going to be disappointed when it doesn't. You can't rely on external factors to be your saving grace—you can't rely on other human beings to reassure you that you are making the right choices. If you become habituated into seeking reassurance from others, you will find yourself blaming all of those around you when it doesn't work out. You will find yourself never taking responsibility for any of your choices or actions. Just trust yourself—just trust that your choices and actions all have a purpose. Whether you realize that purpose in this very moment is to be said, but there will come a time when you realize that purpose. Just stop constantly seeking reassurance and have a little faith. Have a little faith that the path you are on is going to lead you to where you were always meant to be. Have a little faith that one way or another, things will work out. Have a little faith that the decisions you are making will impact your life positively. Realize that no one truly has the answer. No one has cracked the code to “life”—so when you seek reassurance from others, just realize you are seeking reassurance from someone who is probably just as in the dark as you. Seeking reassurance is nothing more than a comforting blanket—it is a weakness that you have fed yourself for years because you were too naive to realize it. It is a poor trait that you have failed to address and now is your time to address it. Seeking reassurance is an easy way to put fault on others—it’s an easy way to not take full responsibility. You have convinced yourself that if you are wrong, it’s okay because someone else is wrong with you—and that gives you comfort. Instead, what you should realize is that no decision is a bad decision if you can learn and grow from it. When you come to terms with that, the need for reassurance will be eliminated. You won’t need to feel validated with your decisions once you firmly believe that the choices you make will only propel you forward. Seeking reassurance constantly only proves that you lack the ability to believe in the one person you should always believe in—yourself. Seeking reassurance only shows others that you lack the ability to make a decision for yourself. How can others trust you to make a decision if you can't even trust yourself to do so? Have some confidence—fall down with some pride if you have to and get right back up. Get rid of this crutch of constantly seeking reassurance because that's all it is.

I want to follow up by saying that there is a clear distinction between constantly seeking reassurance and asking others for some guidance. The distinction lies in becoming unable to make a confident decision for yourself. When you seek reassurance consistently, you fall into the habit of not being able to make life choices, or at the very least, having an extremely difficult time making life choices. Asking for guidance on the other hand is receiving knowledge or perspective from another individual with the intent of making a final decision for yourself. You are allowed to seek guidance from others, in fact, I encourage it, and at some points in your life you may need some validation to help make a decision, but it's when you constantly seek reassurance that it becomes an issue. You cannot lose a grasp on the ability to make a decision for yourself. There is nothing wrong with asking others for help, but you cannot become reliant on them to dictate your path in life. You cannot become powerless in the ability to help yourself. You should not feel guilty if you seek some reassurance during some points in your life, just be mindful when seeking reassurance becomes habitual. Be mindful when seeking reassurance becomes a crutch or a comforting blanket. Seek guidance—not constant reassurance.

Here's a helpful tip:

Instead of asking someone if you made the right decision, ask them why the decision made was or was not the right one.

Do you think I made the right decision? vs. Why do you think the decision I made was or was not the right one?

The first question leads to a yes or no answer, while the second question leads to an answer with some insight. The first question looks for an answer that provides comfort, while the second question looks for an answer that provides growth. The first question gravitates towards reassurance, while the second question gravitates towards guidance. Do you see where I'm going with this? Simply learning to rephrase how a question is asked will help break the habit of constantly seeking reassurance. The first question expresses uncertainty—it demonstrates an inability to take full responsibility for the decision. The second question portrays ownership in the decision made—there is a call to action to receive an outside perspective with the intent of enhancing the ability to make decisions in the future. Try this tip to help shift your mindset.

The day I went into atrial fibrillation and was transported by ambulance to the hospital, I kept asking the paramedics if I was going to die. I mean, not for anything, my heart was beating upwards of 180 beats per minute at rest and I had gone into a state of hyperventilation. I knew I wasn't going to die though—I knew I wasn't having a heart attack. As a practitioner, I assessed myself and called the ambulance suspicious of going into atrial fibrillation—and I was right. Yet, I kept seeking reassurance from others to know that way worse wasn't happening. I completely disregarded all of my knowledge and my instinct as a healthcare provider as I fell into the depths of my self-doubt. Maybe I'm being hard on myself, but I'm going to prove a point. At that moment I succumbed to my worry. When I arrived at the hospital, I must have asked the ER nurses and physicians about 10+ times if I was going to die (especially when they had to cardiovert me). I knew the process, and I knew what it entailed, yet I needed to hear that I was going to be okay. When I asked if I was going to die in the ambulance, I knew the answer was no, not because medically there were no signs indicating that, but because I knew that there was no way they would say yes even if I was (at least in that very moment). So why ask? Why ask a question I already knew the answer to? Was the feeling of being reassured that important? Looking back on that moment is interesting to think about. It made me realize that, like myself at that moment, many seek reassurance for the sole purpose of feeling comfort, regardless of already knowing the answer. Some of us even rather be told a lie for the sake of putting our minds at ease. While my incident may be an extreme example, my point is that you cannot rely on others to put your mind at ease—you need to have that power. Get rid of self-doubt. Yeah, I was under extreme stress while being transported in an ambulance, but I let that overcome me to the point I negated everything I knew as a healthcare provider. At that moment, I let myself become powerless and I didn't need to. People let stress, worry, fear, frustration, etc. cloud their judgment to the point they seek reassurance. So, while seeking constant reassurance is something I've worked on, and even though this scenario is rather extreme, I realized that there was something deeper rooted within that situation. That situation demonstrated that even under the most extreme type of stress, I need to learn to be stronger for myself. It showed me that when life takes a turn, I need to stick to what I know and what I feel. When life takes a turn I just need to have a little faith—I hope I can encourage others to do the same.

As a society, we crave instant gratification. We have forgotten what it feels like to enjoy the anticipation, to enjoy the wait, and to embrace the process—we constantly want results, but we neglect the process. Love the journey as much as the destination. Become addicted to the process—truly become obsessed with it. Become obsessed with getting after your day. Become consumed with being better. Wake up early—maximize the amount of time you can utilize to be better. Stay disciplined—construct a plan and stick to it. Enjoy every bit of the process and more importantly, do it for you. Realize that this journey is between you and you. Results will come in time, but for now, live in the moment. Embrace the daily grind—truly fall in love with it. Results become that much more attainable when you begin to fall in love with the grind. Stop looking so far ahead in life—you are missing the opportunities that are right in front of you. You are blind to the tiny battles you face daily because you are so focused on the end game. Win those tiny battles—overcome daily obstacles. Be proud of the small wins as the small wins are a pivotal part of the process. These small wins will compound over time, creating bigger and bigger wins. Start chipping away at your goals and live for doing so. There is no need to be so consumed with the results amid the process. Life becomes so much more enjoyable when you begin to embrace the process. Stop stressing about hitting certain milestones at certain times. Goals give you direction, but they don't need to be the end all be all. Accept that life happens—different variables are going to be thrown your way, variables that may significantly impact your plan and end goal. You can either stress about it or you can take it as an opportunity to enjoy the process even more.

Become obsessed with bettering yourself—become obsessed with positive action. You gain the advantage during moments everyone else feels like resting. You gain the advantage during moments everyone else feels like giving up, but not you—you keep going because you are obsessed with being the best version of yourself. Have the mentality to just keep pushing forward—to just keep going and never quit. Create momentum and never let it stop—let the fire within you continue to burn. So many individuals would love to be in the position you are in, so don't take life for granted and take advantage of every opportunity thrown your way. Quitting is never an option. I repeat, quitting is never an option. Any task that you are given, attack it with full force and to the best of your ability. This life can be cutthroat—some may say life is the biggest competitive event there is, but you can't approach life with the intent to compete with others. Just compete with yourself and let the rest unfold as it may. As long as you compete with yourself and continue to improve upon who you once were, you will continuously have the advantage. The more you become obsessed with bettering yourself, the more of an advantage you will have in this life.

The next time you feel like quitting, remember that the effort you are putting in now is going to set you up for a bright future. Your actions each day have an impact on the future that lies ahead. You are going to be presented with plenty of choices in this life and you're going to have to make plenty of decisions, so make sure you make the right ones. And if you don't, do not quit—learn from your mistakes and grow. You can never quit—you must always finish what you started. Have a sense of pride—you owe it to yourself to never quit and to set your future self up for success. Times may feel tough right now, they may feel challenging, and they may even feel pointless, but trust the fact that the effort you are putting forth is all worth it. Years from now you will be thanking yourself for all of the hard work you put forth. You will look back on those sleepless nights, those days practicing for countless hours, or the additional time spent in your workplace, all of which may have seemed frustrating at the time, and you'll thank yourself. You will be proud of yourself for never quitting and for constantly believing in yourself. You will be happy in the end to know that all it took was an effort—an effort to make a difference, an effort to grow, and an effort to never give up. That's all it ever takes—just a little effort. Yet, people struggle to put forth effort—to try, to the best of their ability. People struggle because mentally they aren't convinced that the effort they are portraying will yield some sort of return. Believe that the time you are putting in now will yield a bright future because it will.

Take yourself out of environments that are not conducive to your growth and success. You cannot allow yourself to get trapped—to get stuck amongst negativity all around you. Do not allow others to bring you down with them. Learn to say no. One of the biggest lessons I have learned to this day is the importance of telling people no. You can't get dragged into other people's messes and you certainly shouldn't feel the need to be the one to clean it up always. Just say no it's that simple. Put yourself into environments that bring you happiness—that allow you to create. Surround yourself with individuals that are going to push you to new heights—individuals that are going to push you to be a better person. Who you surround yourself with and the environments you constantly find yourself in truly have an impact on your overall well-being—your mood, your drive, and your desires. Eliminate the distractions—figure out who and what does not supplement your life in any way. Make note of the aspects in your life that are not propelling you towards your goals and dreams—

make note of the aspects holding you back with the firmest grip. Maybe it's your current workplace. Maybe it's your current group of friends—side note if those you consider your friends aren't constantly pushing you to grow, then it's time to reconsider if they're friends or simply just acquaintances. Maybe it's where you are currently living. I don't know and only you can be the determinant of that, but what I do know is that the longer you wait to make note of what is holding you back, the more difficult it will be to get unstuck. Do not allow yourself to get stuck. You have the freedom to do whatever it is that brings you joy so just go do it. There is no reason to stay right where you are at this point in your life if you truly believe it is not where you are supposed to be. Time is finite and it is ticking. The longer you wait to take yourself out of environments that are not conducive to your growth and success, the more guilt and regret you will have to live with that you did not do it sooner. No one deserves to live with guilt and regret. No one deserves to have to look back and wish they got out when they could have. You do not want to be that person that looks back on your life wishing that you spent your time more appropriately—wishing that you put yourself into environments that would have brought you more joy. You do not want to be that person that looks back and questions why you surrounded yourself with those that never really added value to your life, that all they did was question your actions and bring you down. That's why it is imperative to make changes now. That's why it is so crucial to make note of who and what is trapping you. Do not live life getting stuck—live life getting free. That's the name of the game.

Don't get stuck—there's always a way out. You can always create opportunities for yourself—it may not be easy, but there is always a way to do so. If you feel like you are at a standstill in your life, go ahead and do something about it. Creating opportunity requires effort—it requires discipline and belief in yourself that you are truly capable of doing so. Don't fear the unknown—just go for it. You cannot become complacent and content with your life just because it is "comfortable"—comfortable does not always equate to happiness. Take risks and bet on yourself, especially if doing so will provide you with a better future—especially if doing so will lead to a happier life. Too often people feel like they cannot advance their life—they feel that they may not have the resources to do so. Some may be more fortunate than others, but every single human being can create opportunities for themselves—they just need to find a way. You must find a way—just figure it out. Many have succeeded and have accomplished greatness with less than what you have. Stop expecting your path to be easy—it's not going to be and regardless, what is the fun in that? Accomplishment is that much more satisfying knowing the trials and tribulations you needed to endure to get to where you wanted to be. You don't need to be stuck where you are. You cannot allow external factors to dictate your future—only you can dictate your future. You are capable of creating opportunities for yourself and you have to do just that.

Give yourself purpose. Give yourself meaning. You can't rely on others to do that for you. You cannot allow yourself to get stuck in an endless loop of complacency—the same boring routine day in and day out that brings you no fulfillment. Try new things—push your boundaries and get uncomfortable. Be creative—utilize your mind in ways that you never have before. What is your purpose in this life? This is an important question to consider. This is a question that you may not have the answer to and here's the crazy part, you may never have an answer. The beauty in that is that if you spend your entire life trying to figure out the answer, you will live a more fulfilled life without even realizing it. Here's the thing, ultimately, it's not about your purpose, rather it's about your actions that you put forth in seeking what your purpose actually is—that is what gives you meaning. Your daily actions, and your efforts consistently to find your purpose, will determine the value you bring to this world. You don't need to focus so hard on defining your purpose with words—let your actions define your purpose. Let your actions give you meaning. Let your actions show the world the value you bring. That's what it is all about—your actions. Words are meaningless until you back them up. Telling others what your purpose is and the value you bring to the table is useless until you back it up with action. If you want to find your purpose, reflect on the actions you put forth daily—reflect on the aspects of life you dedicate your energy towards. Reflect on the outcomes of your actions—do they impact you and those around you positively? What you do daily determines your purpose and meaning in life. Your daily actions are the value you bring to this world, so think about whether your actions today provided any value—to yourself and those around you. When you start to approach life trying to maximize your days, trying to utilize every second to provide some sort of value to yourself and those around you, that is when you will begin to get clarity on what your purpose in life is. That is when you will begin to feel like your life truly has meaning. But remember, it's not so much about what your purpose is, but more so your path to finding your purpose. Think of this rationale from the perspective of mathematics. No one cares about the answer—they care about how you got the answer. They care about how you solved the equation or how you came up with the solution. People want to see the work—they want to see the efforts it took to obtain the results. So, when you ask yourself what is your purpose in life, remember it's okay to not have the answer because you are in the process of solving the equation. As long as you are living, you may never have a concrete answer, but you will get more and more clarity as life goes on. The process holds more weight than the result yielded. The blueprint holds more value than the finished product. Approach life with this in mind—watch how much happier and fulfilled you feel.

Let your actions define your purpose.

Everyone copes differently. Everyone handles situations differently. You are in no place to judge someone on how they are handling a situation. You handle situations in ways that are specific to you—ways that may not be conventional to the "norm." We as humans possess an array of emotions—we battle internal struggles day in and day out. How individuals cope with such struggles should be respected by you and those around you—as I can imagine you would want the same respect for yourself. Too often people are quick to judge the actions of others, rather than taking a second to think about what that individual may be going through. People often just look at what is happening superficially rather than what is happening deep within the minds and souls of others. Some people do "weird" things when they're going through a tough time, but what is "weird" to you might not be "weird" to them. I'm sure during your moments of loss, sadness, and anger you've acted in ways that many would find odd, but ultimately those ways helped you overcome an obstacle. You are allowed to cope in your own way and shouldn't fear the judgment of others. Live life the way you want to live it. Handle loss the way you want to handle it. Overcome sadness the way you want to overcome it. There's no rule book on how to handle these situations—there's no golden rule on what to do in moments of despair.

It's not a matter of what is right or what is wrong. It's a matter of doing what you feel is right. It's a matter of doing what you believe in. You can't sit there contemplating your choices every single time one needs to be made. You can't sit there regretting choices made and actions that were already conducted. You made a decision because that is what you felt was right at that moment—so move on and stop second-guessing it. Social norms will only take you so far—your choices shouldn't be dictated by what others would do. Make a decision based on your morals, your ethics, and your values. You shouldn't live life solely based on what is accepted by society—you will find yourself lost in an abyss of uncertainty because that's all life really is. Life is one big uncertain path and while you may think others have it figured out, they don't. No one truly knows what's right and what's wrong—we just create this construct of what is accepted and what isn't. There will be times in your life when you will be faced with a decision, one that you feel is right, yet isn't accepted by most. Those are the times you truly need to stick to your morals, your ethics, and your values. Those are the times to question if you and those around you will benefit from the decision you are about to make. There have been instances where lives were saved because someone made a decision that many would not or such a decision went against what is accepted in society. Heroes are born because they do not contemplate what is right and what is wrong—they just do. They follow their moral compass and stick to what they believe in. They seek to bring a greater good to humanity. That's what you need to do—think less and just do. Think less about what is right and what is wrong—do more of what you believe in. You are going to make mistakes. You are going to make decisions that you felt in those moments were the ones to be made but ended up being the "wrong" ones. That is how you learn—that is how you grow. That is how you become a better human being. Every single day is a lesson, so start treating it that way. More lessons will be learned when you start living life doing what you believe in. There will be more self-growth when you stop overthinking, overanalyzing, and contemplating every single choice that comes your way. Instead, contrary to what you have been accustomed to, just do—don't think, just act. Overthinking choices that need to be made just weighs you down. The contemplation just creates unwarranted stress or anxiety. Just trust your gut and follow your instinct. You will find yourself way less concerned with what is right and what is wrong when you start to trust your gut. What is right and what is wrong will not matter because you will be doing what you feel is right—that's what matters. Life needs to be lived this way. You will find yourself living a more fulfilled and stress-free life when you stop worrying so much about the choices you are making. Just do—do what you feel is right.

Creation brings upon happiness and happiness brings upon creation—it's an infinite loop. There's just something about bringing an idea to life that is so rewarding. Creation brings this sense of freedom. When creating, you have full autonomy to go in any direction you desire. You have full ownership over your ideas and with such ideas, you can help others. You can inspire others and bring others happiness. We live in a world where the ability to create is made easy—we have all of the resources right at our fingertips. Creating doesn't need to involve the latest and greatest technology—you can create with a pen and a piece of paper. All you need is an idea and it snowballs from there. I love creating, whether it's writing, educating, or filming, I genuinely love creating. Life would be so boring if it wasn't for the freedom to create—life would be so bland. The ability to create allows you to be yourself—it allows you to project to the world your inner self. The ability to create allows you to turn your thoughts into reality—it allows you to communicate to others in ways deeper than typical dialect. Many struggle to communicate with others and through creation that is made easy—there is something special in that. How a piece of art can convey a message—how a book or an article from a journal can connect to thousands of individuals to their deepest core. The connection and impact you have on others through creation, which many times remains unknown, is what makes creating worthwhile. It's not about recognition. It's not about being noticed. It's about the impact you can have on others while remaining in the dark—your creativity is what brings the light. Your creativity can have a lifelong lasting impact on those that come across your creation. You can change someone's life for the better without ever meeting that individual. Now, that's something to be grateful for. No one can ever take away your ability to create—no one can determine the value of your creations besides you. You are the ultimate determinant of the value of all that it is you create and that's all that should matter.

Those that are the happiest creating are the ones that do so without fearing judgment. Those that are the happiest creating do so because it simply brings joy to them. Creating allows you to open up and free your mind—it allows you to get rid of all of the weight you feel like you are holding on to. When you are creating, nothing else should matter at that moment—nothing else does matter at that moment. When you are creating, you are truly free.

"The idea is not to live forever, it is to create something that will." — Andy Warhol

Sometimes you need to just give yourself a break. Remind yourself that it's okay to relax and unwind—to *rest* as described earlier. Furthermore, you shouldn't feel guilty about taking a break from reality—from taking a break from the hard work you put in daily. You shouldn't feel guilty about going out, watching a television series, or eating dessert at your favorite restaurant. You're allowed to live your life. It only becomes problematic when you start overindulging in activities that aren't productive or don't add any value. I have seen too many individuals, including myself, become so critical of themselves simply because they wanted to give themselves a break. Yes, you should be obsessed with the process of being better and you should fall in love with the daily grind, but don't let that obsession destroy you. I will forever promote individuals to work their hardest and to maximize their potential daily, but such individuals need to find balance. Finding balance is truly the key to living a happy and successful life. The process, or challenge, of finding this balance is what makes life exciting. Finding this balance is person specific—there is no specific blueprint for it, but what remains consistent is having to determine what is important to you and what is detrimental to you. Everything in between will depend on the individual and the goals of that individual. There are plenty of ways to give yourself a break without being or becoming lazy. There are plenty of ways to give yourself a break without losing progress. A lot of it has to do with discipline—the discipline to remain focused and not lose sight of what is important in life. If you can stay disciplined, motivated, and consistent day in and day out, then you will have an easier time finding balance. Find this balance or you're going to have a difficult time truly enjoying life. Working in healthcare can be stressful, just like many of the fields others work in can be. There are moments when I just need a break from the seriousness of everything happening in life—a break from the seriousness of my field of work. Sometimes that break just happens to consist of watching the latest television series. Should I feel guilty about doing that? There was a time I would feel guilty for doing just that, but I reminded myself of the number of hours I spent working so hard, not just at my job, but to maintain good physical health, good mental health, and good spiritual health. I found balance because I was able to stay disciplined in maximizing the areas in life that were important to me while not letting that obsession in doing so destroy me. The point is, you cannot get lost in the process of maximizing your potential and you should not be so hard on yourself. You are allowed to enjoy life and escape reality for a bit—again, just don't overindulge in activities that aren't productive or don't add any value. Enjoy going out, enjoy the latest television series, and enjoy the dessert, but don't lose sight of the important aspects of your life. Don't lose sight of your non-negotiables.

While it's great to be organized and regimented, being too organized and too regimented can be detrimental. I say this because it can lead you to panic when chaos ensues. It can lead you to struggle when having to navigate through obstacles in life. It can lead you to fear going with the flow. So, while you may be organized and regimented, remember that life around you may not be—and usually is not. There are going to be days when you have to completely shift gears and go off course. Be flexible. Learn to constantly adapt. People tend to struggle with this. They struggle because they fear change. They struggle because they have become so conditioned to a specific daily regimen that anything other than their routine just feels uncomfortable. You can't allow yourself to fear change—teach yourself to embrace the lack of comfort and thrive in it. Learn that every aspect of life will not be approached in the same manner and doesn't have to be approached in the same manner. Be willing to put yourself out there and try new things—go off course once in a while. Explore the uncomfortable—explore outside of what your daily regimen consists of. That's how you get stronger—that's how you grow as an individual. Be organized and regimented, but be willing to adapt regarding all aspects of life. You will not succeed if you cannot bring yourself to embrace change. You will not succeed if you cannot convince yourself to be flexible. Not for anything, do you want to live a life performing the same routine over and over again? You should love when you have to navigate obstacles—you should love when challenges are thrown your way. That's what makes life exciting—that's what makes life fulfilling and worthwhile. Not only should you train yourself to better handle situations that require adaptation, but you should look forward to it. When you learn to embrace the chaos, happiness will increase and your success with anything in life will increase. When you learn to embrace the chaos, you will truly start to feel unstoppable. Embrace the chaos—you will feel as though there is nothing that can prevent you from moving forward with your day in a positive manner.

Share your knowledge—share your insight with the world. You truly have so much to offer to those around you. You have the capability of motivating and inspiring—utilize that gift. Continue to be authentic. You don't need to be like anyone else to succeed—you just need to continue to be you. Many seek what you can offer. You see, your knowledge is something that can never be taken away from you. What you possess in your mind is yours. When all is said and done, our mind is all we ever really have. If you want to truly impact those around you, start by offering your knowledge—share the education that was bestowed upon you with others. Your knowledge, your ability to educate, is drastically more useful than any materialistic object you could offer someone. The spreading of knowledge is a domino effect—one life impacts another, that impacts another, and so on. The next thing you know, your insight has impacted an entire network of individuals. The beauty in sharing knowledge is that there truly isn't any information that can be deemed not useful. Any information that is shared with you can be utilized to some degree. What you may find as being useless may just be eye-opening on what not to do or what route not to take—that is certainly useful. Anytime a message is conveyed to you, you should look to dissect what is being conveyed—you should analyze and see what part of that information can positively benefit your life. Too often people listen to information and immediately resort to believing it does not apply to their life. I will say it again, all information can be useful to some degree if you put the effort and belief into the fact that it will be. On the flip side of this, many are hesitant to share their knowledge because they have convinced themselves that what they want to convey to others is useless.

Your knowledge, your message, and the information you possess are useful—it's useful to many more individuals than you think. At the end of the day, if you can impact just one human being, then that should be enough for you—that should be enough to convince you that the knowledge you possess is beneficial.

I think one of my biggest fears is not being remembered. I want to have an ever-lasting impact on the world. I want to shape the minds of others. This fear fuels me—it fuels me to work hard, learn more, and take risks. I can't go through this life not making a difference—no matter how big or small. Life is short, and life is uncertain, but life is full of opportunities—take advantage of those opportunities. Maximize every single day because the next day is not guaranteed. Don't fear the unknown—embrace it. Embrace the unknown with open arms and just go for it—go for whatever it is that brings you happiness, joy, and fulfillment. Leave your mark on this world. Don't be afraid to shake things up a bit. Don't be afraid to stand out.

Don't be afraid period. Fear is fuel—fuel to make a change, to motivate, and to inspire. Everyone deserves to be remembered—it just takes effort. More importantly, it takes being yourself. Don't blend in with the crowd—be you. Be the person you were meant to be and if you're not quite sure who that is, continue searching because that is what life is all about. Life is about finding who you are and enjoying the process. The process is what gets you remembered. The process is what holds the most value. Your process is unique—your path in life cannot be replicated. Are you making the most out of your process? Are you making the most out of your journey through life? Are you putting forth effort daily to be the best version of yourself—the version that those will remember once you are long gone? Let the fear of not being remembered fuel you. Go out and make a difference in this world.

I once feared that everything I wanted and desired in this life would not come to fruition—that it simply would not happen regardless of how hard I worked. I once feared that all I ever wanted to accomplish would be an impossible feat because it just wasn't in the cards for me. The future worried me and I feared all of my efforts would be for nothing. Then came a day that I realized I can't live life like that—I can't live life worrying about what has yet to come. I convinced myself that if I truly want something in this life and I truly work at it, then it will happen. I firmly believe this to be true. YOU need to believe this to be true—the best has yet to come.

Be remembered.

THE JOURNEY NEVER ENDS

It's crazy to think that everything I've felt or experienced led me to this very instance. That all of those times of stress, frustration, and anger led to something great—this written text. Those moments that could have been conveyed as negative led to a positive outcome. So, while during those moments I was hard on myself, I should have realized that maybe, just maybe, it would all work out. That's what I've come to learn and that's what I hope you can get out of this. I hope this written text will help change the way you think. I hope you learn to cherish those stressful moments because something good will come out of them. More importantly, don't forget about the good times. Cherish the moments of happiness, love, and achievement, as they are all playing a role in your story too. Everything truly happens for a reason—it's only a matter of time until you realize that reason.

www.ingramcontent.com/pod-product-compliance
Lightning Source LLC
La Vergne TN
LVHW010612100826
845148LV00014B/2933

9798218217945